Pierre A. Caron de Beaumarchais

THE BARBER OF

and

THE MARRIAGE

TRANSLATED FROM THE FRENCH AND
WITH AN INTRODUCTION BY
Vincent Luciani PH.D
The City College
The City University of New York

Barron's Educational Series, inc.

SEVILLE

OF FIGARO

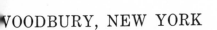

WOODBURY, NEW YORK

INTRODUCTION

Beaumarchais

Pierre Augustin Caron de Beaumarchais was born in Paris, January 24, 1732, the year of George Washington's birth. His father, a watchmaker by trade, belonged to the Roman Catholic faith, although his family before him was Calvinistic. Of his four sons Pierre was the only one who survived, and so, naturally, his father destined him to be a watchmaker. Up to the age of thirteen, young Pierre attended a sort of technical school at Alfort. The merry wine shops of the Halles were too much for Pierre, who had a gay, vivacious bent. Like Chérubin and Figaro, he liked women and song, but his father extracted from him a promise that he would be industrious in his work and exemplary in his conduct. After this, the young man so applied himself to the trade of watchmaker that at twenty he invented a new escapement. A tiny ring watch made by him for Madame de Pompadour was much admired by Louis XV and introduced its maker to the court.

In 1757 Pierre married a widow Madame Franquet, who, although pretty, was ten years his senior and died soon thereafter. From her Caron acquired the title of De Beaumarchais. But Pierre's skill on the harp brought him closer to the royal family, for he taught that instrument to Louis XV's daughters. At about this time Beaumarchais became connected with the famous financier Paris-Duverney, who interested him in some of his enterprises. To rise to a higher station in life, Caron paid 56,000 livres for the title of *secrétaire du roi*.

Like his Figaro, he liked schemes. A sister of his had gone to Madrid and had become affianced to a certain Spanish man of letters, Clavijo by name. After the bans of marriage had been published, Clavijo disappeared. Beaumarchais hastened to Spain (1764), made the disloyal suitor avow his guilt, and also made him promise to marry. But again Clavijo disappeared. Beaumarchais secured an audience with the king and explained the whole case to him. This resulted in Clavijo's disgrace and his dismissal from office. Goethe used the story in his play *Clavigo und Stella* (1774). On the trip to Spain, Beaumarchais was also the secret agent of Duverney, who sought in the peninsula a field for his vast financial schemes. Here in Spain, Beaumarchais attempted to get the contract for supplying the Spanish colonies with negro slaves, elaborated a plan to stimulate manufactures in the peninsula, negotiated the granting of Louisiana trade to a French syndicate, and to improve friendly relations between Spain and France, succeeded in getting the French Marquise de la Croix accepted as the Spanish king's favorite. In the midst of these activities he found time to become interested in the music, dances, and drama of Spain, an interest which he showed later in his comedies.

In 1765, he returned to Paris, where he spent his leisure moments writing plays. Under the influence of the English Richardson and the French Diderot, he wrote *Eugénie*, which proved to be a dismal failure the first night, but which the author so changed that it became for some time a great success. Encouraged by this, Beaumarchais composed another *drame, The Two Friends*, dealing with a financial and commercial venture. It had only an indifferent success, but fortunately his next two plays are among the masterpieces of the French theatre. In 1768, Beaumarchais married again, this time also a pretty widow, Madame Lévêque, whose death, three years later, gave his enemies the opportunity to repeat the charge that he had used poison.

In 1770 Paris-Duverney died, bequeathing his entire fortune to his nephew, the Comte de la Blache, and declaring Beaumarchais free of all indebtedness. In fact, he stated that he himself owed the latter 15,000 livres. La Blache, who cordially detested his uncle's friend, contested the will and went to court, which ruled in 1772 in favor of Beaumarchais. La Blache then appealed. A dispute with the Duc de Chaulnes over a young actress led to a big fight which put the two principals in jail. Beaumarchais was sent to the prison of For-l'Évêque, given only permission to visit his judges. In April 1773, the decision of the lower court was reversed, thanks to the report of counsellor Goëzman. Beaumarchais had to pay La Blache 56,000 livres, plus the interest for five years, and the costs. He in part avenged himself with his *Theses against Goëzman,* pamphlets characterized by their sardonic wit. Voltaire praised the first three. When the fourth and best *Thesis* appeared, the public went wild.

Notwithstanding Beaumarchais's popularity, he lost his civic rights and his *Theses* were condemned to be publically burned. In order to be rehabilitated, he appealed to Louis XV, but to no avail, because the king was approaching his end. Louis XVI, who had no reason to be grateful to Beaumarchais, used him to advantage when a libellous pamphlet against Marie Antoinette was about to appear in London. After some thrilling adventures of Beaumarchais, the libel was not published. On his return to Paris, he succeeded in having the Comédie Française undertake the rehearsals of the comedy, *The Barber of Seville,* which was finally produced on February 23, 1775. The first performance was a dismal failure, but the author combined the fourth and fifth acts and made other modifications so that it became a tremendous success.

Meanwhile Beaumarchais continued to be Louis XVI's agent in suppressing libellous pamphlets. He thus won the king's confidence and favor, and in 1776 he was restored to his civil status and former offices. During one of his affairs in London, he had watched the struggle between England and her American colonies and had proposed to the

French government a means of furnishing arms and sup-
plies to the rebels. His plans were encouraged, but all dealings with America had to be, he was told, in the nature of
a secret alliance. Therefore, he readied himself to supply
the Americans with much needed equipment, and was to
receive in repayment cargoes of merchandise. A company
was formed under an assumed name with its offices in Paris.
Its relations were with Silas Dean, agent of the rebels. Another American, Arthur Lee by name, feeling that he was
being supplanted, denounced Beaumarchais to Congress,
accusing him of cheating the colonists. From this calumny
came all the difficulties Beaumarchais had in recovering
payment from the United States.

Beaumarchais contrived in the meantime to have the
verdict in the La Blache case reversed (July 1778) at Aix
in Provence, thanks partly to his *Theses.* In 1779 he engaged in publishing a complete edition of Voltaire's works,
and, as they were prohibited in France, so he used the
printing presses of Kehl. Despite various difficulties, the
Voltaire edition, begun in 1783, was finished in 1790, but
it turned out to be a bad speculation because too few sub-
scribers to each set of books were secured. At this time he
was interested in sundry other projects, yet in the midst of
this activity, he had found time to compose *The Marriage
of Figaro,* probably completed in 1778, accepted three years
later by the Comédie Française, but not acted until 1784.
It was quite an event, and Beaumarchais witnessed its triumph. Sixty-eight performances of the comedy, almost fol-

lowing one another, did not dull the public's enthusiasm for it. Naturally, our author's enemies, especially Suard, were quick to attack the play, but this did not prevent its being popular.

From this year on, Beaumarchais's fame declines. He incurred the wrath of Mirabeau, and a young Provençal lawyer, Bergasse, wrote many pamphlets against him. In 1786 he married Mademoiselle Willermaula, by whom he had a daughter six years before. In 1787 appeared his new opera *Tarare*, with music by Salieri. Although Beaumarchais's libretto does not do honor to the theme, the piece had some success. At about this time he built a sumptuous mansion opposite the Bastille, hoping to occupy it in 1791. But in these days of the Revolution, it was extremely dangerous for one associated with the *ancien régime*. The quarter near the Bastille was very turbulent. Yet in the midst of these conditions, he completed *The Guilty Mother* (1792), the least effective of the Figaro trilogy. Despite its inferiority, the play, thanks to its fourth act, enjoyed a moderate success.

Just before the performance of *The Guilty Mother*, Beaumarchais had obtained 60,000 muskets in Holland for the French government. The difficulty was to deliver them, for Austria, who had sold the guns, had stipulated that they were to be sent to the colonies. Despite his many efforts, Beaumarchais could not get the weapons released by Holland, and he was denounced by French patriots before the

National Assembly (1792). His house was searched, and although nothing incriminating was found, he was led off to prison. Only the intercession of a former mistress saved his life. He entreated Danton to help him. Danton sent him to Holland. Beaumarchais later went to England, where he was imprisoned for debt. While in prison, he wrote his bold *Dissertation on the Six Epochs,* which he distributed on his return to Paris. The arms were never delivered to France. Beaumarchais's name was now put on the list of émigrés, his property was confiscated, his wife, his sister, and his daughter were sent to prison, and only the end of the Reign of Terror saved them from the guillotine. Beaumarchais spent three years in exile. He did not come back to France until the Directory supplanted the Convention in 1796. He exerted himself to restore his shattered fortunes and succeeded in part. On the night of May 17, 1799, he passed away quietly in his sleep, and was buried in his garden. When his house was demolished, his remains were transferred to the cemetery of Père-Lachaise.

Even the above brief sketch of Beaumarchais's life can reveal the main traits of his character. His was a very complex nature. Inordinately ambitious and a great lover of intrigue, he had no moral scruples. Nevertheless, he was capable of true joy, true goodness, true sensitivity, true enthusiasm, and true generosity. He was a good son and a good father. He is the author of two plays that will long exist in our repertories.

Beaumarchais and the Drama

Of the many plays written in the eighteenth century, which was known for its exposition of ideas, very few deserve a lasting reputation. Tragedy had greatly deteriorated, mostly because of the imitation of Racine. Except for some by Voltaire, tragedies of the period were either colorless or bombastic. In comedy things were much better, thanks to Destouches's plays, Lesage's *Turcaret,* and Marivaux's *The Game of Love and Chance,* but they suffered by comparison with Molière of the seventeenth century. Realizing that there was a certain decline in the theatre and that a revival was needed, some created a new form, the *drame* or *comédie larmoyante.* Diderot, the main theorist of this school, had various plays of this kind. His *Natural Son* and *Father of a Family* were dismal failures. Only Sedaine, with his *Philosopher Without Knowing It* (1765), gave the true masterpiece of the *genre.*

Then came Beaumarchais, a name to be placed near Molière's. At first he too joined the ranks of those who wrote *comédies larmoyantes.* The result was *Eugénie* and *The Two Friends,* after which he composed the famous comedies. *The Barber of Seville* is for the most part a comedy of intrigue, not a comedy of character (in which Molière excelled). Its personages are the conventional types of the *commedia dell' arte* and are similar to Molière's *Ecole des femmes:* the lover, the *ingénue,* the guardian in love, the servant. On the surface, it is the usual story of an old man duped, but there is a vital difference.

In order the better to ape Parisian customs, Beaumarchais gives his play a Spanish setting. Count Almaviva, who has been in love with Rosine ever since he met her in Madrid, is waiting beneath her window when he sees Figaro. The latter tells his story after leaving the Count's service, is now a barber in Seville, and lodges in Doctor Bartholo's house. The artful Rosine manages to get a letter to the Count which tells him who she is. From Figaro the Count learns all about Bartholo and don Bazile, Rosine's music teacher, who is taking care of arrangements for Bartholo's forthcoming wedding to Rosine. The old guardian wants so much to marry his young ward. The first act is a good exposition: it introduces all the characters and tells us what each of them is desirous of having. In the subsequent acts the scene shifts to Bartholo's house. Rosine wants to learn from Figaro what he knows about Lindor, the name the Count has assumed. She finds out that she is loved by him. Meanwhile the barber has crippled Bartholo's household, the better to foster the Count's plans. Soon after don Bazile comes to see Bartholo and tell him that Almaviva has settled in Seville. It is then that Bazile makes his famous speech on slander, which has thrilled audiences for close to two centuries. When Bazile leaves, the Count comes in, disguised as a drunken trooper who has obtained permission to lodge in the house for one night, but as soon as he hears that Bartholo has been exempted from billeting, he departs. The ensuing scene attests to Bartholo's jealousy and Rosine's shrewdness. Act II thus ends. It is the longest in a play of four acts. The Count, now disguised as Alonzo, Bazile's pupil, says that Bazile is ill, worms his way into Bartholo's confidence, and gives a music lesson to Rosine. She insists on singing *The Useless Precaution,* while Bartholo listens. Figaro comes in to shave him. Bazile arrives, but before he can talk against Alonzo, he leaves, aided in part by the Count's persuasive argument (money). The latter tells Rosine that they have stolen the key of her blinds. Bartholo learns that Alonzo is not Bazile's pupil and tries to shake Rosine's confidence in Lindor. She believes that he is involved in a conspiracy with Count Almaviva. Not knowing that Lindor and Almaviva are one and the same, she thinks she is going to become the Count's mistress. Therefore, she consents then and there to marry Bartholo, but Almaviva easily persuades her and weds her. The contract is signed, and Rosine becomes the Countess Almaviva.

From this brief summary *The Barber of Seville* does not seem to be an unusual play, but there is at least one creation, the barber. Figaro is not the ordinary valet. He is a true Parisian, he is not Mascarille, Scapin or the many servants of the Italian Renaissance. He serves his master, but he has many talents. He is a poet, an author, a writer for newspapers, a Jack of all trades, and above all, a schemer. The character of Figaro and Beaumarchais's dialogue help to make *The Barber of Seville* a great play. This dialogue, especially when Figaro speaks, is different. It is the surprise of the comedy. Lanson says in his *History of French Literature:* "It is the supreme perfection of the spirit of conversation: a constant crackle of ingenious, mordant, droll words, flashes of tirades, a rattle of opposing rejoinders; the mind is filled, dazzled, stunned, astonished by them." The characters are great talkers, even that rascal Bazile. Beaumarchais's verve is regulated, directed, conscious. He put everything of value in *The Barber* and *The Marriage.*

The Marriage of Figaro is much longer than *The Barber of Seville,* has five acts instead of four, and its action is not so concentrated. It's dialogue is even more serious, above all where Figaro is concerned. It too is a comedy of intrigue, bordering on the comedy of manners rather than that of character. Figaro reappears in *The Marriage.* He had a few barbs against the *ancien régime* and the nobility in *The Barber,* but here he became identified in the minds of the populace with the champion of liberty and equality against tyranny and privilege. This would-be child of the Revolution is truly the main character of the play. Beaumarchais also adheres to the Spanish milieu, although the personages are obviously French. All the action of the comedy takes place in Count Almaviva's castle in Aguas-Frescas, near Seville.

The day of the wedding has finally arrived. Figaro, who is measuring the room he is to occupy with his bride-to-be Suzanne, learns from her that the Count wishes to make her his mistress. Marceline, an older woman who prides herself on being quite a wit, also loves Figaro and Suzanne knows it. Chérubin, a mere child in love with love, tells the latter that he was surprised with Fanchette by the Count, who in turn told him to leave the castle. At just about this time Almaviva visits Suzanne, even though she does nothing to encourage him. Chérubin hides behind an armchair. After a while the Count perceives him and pardons him upon the insistence of the Countess and others, on condition that he depart immediately for Catalonia as a captain in his regiment. Figaro, however, tells him to come back. This first act does not introduce all the characters. Brid'oison, Antonio, and Grippe-Soleil do not appear. Figaro has a plan to expose the Count's jealousy and philandering. He has had Bazile give his lordship an anonymous note informing him that some gallant will try to pay court to the Countess during the dance, and he tells Suzanne to accept a rendezvous with the Count that evening. Only he is going to substitute Chérubin for her. When Figaro leaves, Chérubin enters. The women try Suzanne's clothes on him, and Suzanne sings with guitar accompaniment Chérubin's ballad in honor of the Countess. Then follow the scenes in which the Count reveals his jealousy. Chérubin jumps into the garden and Suzanne takes his place. Antonio, however, has seen a man come out of the window. Figaro tells the Count that he is that fellow, although Antonio cannot believe it. The Count is going to London as ambassador. At first he wants to take Figaro along as the King's Messenger and Suzanne as a sort of ambassadress (but actually as his mistress), but when she refuses, he has misgivings about Figaro because he does not know English. It is then that the latter makes his exaggerated speeches about "God-damn" and politics. Afterwards come the court scenes which introduce the stutterer Brid'oison and which testify to Beaumarchais's experience in lawsuits. Marceline, who has lent Figaro some money, wins the case and is expected to marry him. The scenes (especially 15 of Act III) are a satire against justice in the *ancien régime*. Shortly thereafter Marceline learns that Figaro is the long lost son that she has had with Bartholo. She endeavors to have Bartholo marry her but he refuses. It is then that she delivers a long discourse on women's rights.

Everybody is happy except the Count. Marceline is going to marry Bartholo after all, and Figaro can now wed his Suzanne. That Chérubin can take the latter's place is out of the question, so Figaro elicits a promise that she will not keep the rendezvous. The Countess, however, has different ideas: she will go in Suzanne's place and the latter writes the Count a note informing him that the meeting will take place under the chestnut trees. Shortly afterwards Antonio and the Count discover Chérubin dressed as a girl. Instead of punishing him, the Count gives him in marriage to Fanchette, according to her desire. The wedding procession can now begin. During the cortège Suzanne slips her note to the Count. Fanchette unwittingly informs Figaro that the billet-doux is from his intended. Naturally, he is stunned and wishes to surprise her under the great chestnuts. Act V, that contains a long soliloquy by Figaro on his life, which happens to be an indictment of the *ancien régime,* is full of misunderstandings, due in part to the Countess's disguise. The upshot is that Figaro and Suzanne are finally wed, and the Count, reconciled with Rosine, makes the best of a bad bargain.

One at least can see from this short synopsis, which hardly does justice to the play, that *The Marriage* is much more complicated than *The Barber.* Beaumarchais is indebted to many writers: to Molière, in general; to Regnard for his intricate plot; to Lesage for his principal character; to Marivaux for his women. *The Marriage* is a mingling of many dramatic traditions: the social satire of Molière, the Italians, the *comédie larmoyante;* the synthesis of a long literary past in which the bad has been rejected and the good utilized. It is, like *The Barber,* epoch-making for its skill in the treatment of plot, its characters, its crisp dialogue, its impudence. It goes much further, however, and is more serious than the earlier masterpiece. It has many more characters (Marceline, Antonio, Chérubin, Brid'-oison, for example), a greater variety of situations, more pictorial effect in its scenes. *The Barber* might be preferred by some because of its simplicity, but *The Marriage* is for those who have subtler tastes. With all its gaiety it is a better picture of life and is the embodiment of a social mood full of tragic possibilities. *The Marriage* may have been a contributing factor to the French Revolution. At any rate, Figaro, who really worked for himself, became the symbol of the days of the "Rights of Man." *The Barber* was set to music by Gioacchino Rossini (1816) and *The Marriage* by Wolfgang Amedeus Mozart (1786).

APRIL, 1964   *Vincent Luciani*

THE BARBER OF SEVILLE

or

THE USELESS PRECAUTION

CHARACTERS

The actors wear ancient Spanish costumes.

COUNT ALMAVIVA,[1] a grandee of Spain, Rosine's unknown lover, appears in the first act in a short satin jacket and breeches; he is wrapped in a large brown mantle or Spanish cape; a black broad-brimmed hat with a colored ribbon around it. In the second act: a horseman's uniform, a mustache, and half-boots. In the third act, dressed as a student, rounded hair; a large ruff on his neck; a short jacket, breeches, stockings, and a priest's mantle. In the fourth act, he is dressed superbly in Spanish style with a rich mantle. Over everything, he wraps himself in a wide brown mantle.

BARTHOLO, a physician, Rosine's guardian: a black, short, buttoned suit, a large wig; a ruff and turned-up cuffs; a black belt, and, when he leaves his house, a long scarlet mantle.

ROSINE, a young lady of noble birth and Bartholo's ward; dressed in Spanish style.

FIGARO, a barber of Seville, dressed like a Spanish beau.[2]

---

[1] *Almaviva in Spanish and poetic Italian means "living soul," "lively soul."*

[2] *Beaumarchais uses the Spanish* majo *"a popular dandy," similar to the familiar* guapo.

His head covered with a hair-net or snood; a white hat with a colored ribbon around it; a silk neckerchief, tied very loosely to his neck; satin waistcoat and breeches, with buttons and button-holes fringed with silver; a large silk belt; garters with hanging tassels on each leg; a glaring short jacket, quite different from the color of the waistcoat; white stockings and gray shoes.

DON BAZILE, organist, Rosine's singing teacher; a black broad-brimmed hat, a short cassock and a long mantle, without a ruff or cuffs.

LA JEUNESSE, an old servant of Bartholo's.

L'ÉVEILLÉ, another of Bartholo's servants, a simple and sleepy boy. Both dressed as Galicians;[3] their hair in pigtails; a chamois-colored vest; wide leather belt with a buckle; blue breeches and short jacket, the sleeves of which open at the shoulders so that they may hang in the back.

A NOTARY.

A SHERIFF,[4] a man of justice, with a long white rod in his hand.

SEVERAL POLICEMEN AND SERVANTS with torches.

The scene is laid in Seville; in the first act, in the street beneath Rosine's window. The remainder of the play is in Doctor Bartholo's house.

[3] *Galicia is a province of Spain, near Portugal.*
[4] *Beaumarchais uses the Spanish* alcalde *and for "policemen,"* alguazils (*Mod. Span.* alguaciles).

ACT ONE

The stage represents a street in Seville, where all the windows are barred.

SCENE I

(*The* COUNT, *alone in a heavy brown cloak and a broad-brimmed hat. He looks at his watch as he walks up and down.*)

COUNT: The morning is not so advanced as I believed. The hour at which she usually shows herself behind her blinds is still far off. No matter; it is better to be too early than to miss the one moment of seeing her. If some pleasant fellow at court could guess that I were one hundred leagues from Madrid, lingering every morning under the windows of a lady to whom I have never spoken, he would take me for a Spaniard of Isabella's time.—Why not? Everyone seeks happiness. Mine is in the heart of Rosine. —What! follow a lady to Seville, when Madrid and the court everywhere offer such easy pleasures? That is the very thing I shun. I am weary of conquests that interest, convenience or vanity is yielding me all the time. It is so sweet to be loved for oneself: and if I could make sure that under this disguise . . . confound this inopportune fellow!

SCENE 2

FIGARO, THE COUNT, *hidden*

FIGARO: (*with a guitar slung across his back by a wide ribbon; he hums merrily, paper and pencil in hand.*)

> Away with sorrow,
> It consumes us.
> Without the fire of good wine
> Inspiring us,
> It reduces us to languish.
> Man, without pleasure,
> Will live in a stupor,
> With good prospects of dying.

That's not so bad, so far, is it?

> With good prospects of dying.
> Wine and indolence
> Shall dispute my heart.

Well no! they do not dispute, they reign together peacefully.

> Shall share my heart.

Does one say *se partagent?* Well, thank goodness, our writers of comic operas are not so particular about that. Nowadays, what is not worth saying we sing. (*He sings.*)

> Wine and indolence
> Shall share my heart.

I should like to finish with something beautiful, brilliant, sparkling, which would look like an idea. (*He kneels to the ground and writes as he sings.*)

> Shall share my heart.
> If one enjoys my affection . . .
> The other is my bliss.

Pshaw! that's flat. It isn't that. I need an opposition, an antithesis.

> If one . . . be my mistress,
> The other . . .

There! I have it! . . .

> The other is my slave.

Well done, Figaro! . . . (*He writes as he sings.*)

> Wine and indolence
> Shall share my heart:
> If one be my mistress,
> The other is my slave.
> The other is my slave.
> The other is my slave.

There, there, when there are accompaniments to it, we shall see now, gentlemen of the cabal,[1] if I know what I'm saying. (*He perceives the* COUNT.) I've seen that priest somewhere. (*He rises.*)

COUNT: (*aside*) I'm sure I know this fellow.

---

[1] *"Gentlemen of the cabal," originally a secret group of advisers to Charles II of England, in France of the 17th and 18th centuries, any mysterious group.*

FIGARO: No, he's no priest. That proud and noble bearing . . .

COUNT: That grotesque figure . . .

FIGARO: I'm not mistaken, it's Count Almaviva.

COUNT: I think this rascal must be Figaro.

FIGARO: One and the same, my lord.

COUNT: You rogue! If you say one word . . .

FIGARO: Yes, I recognize you; these are the same familiar kindnesses with which you have always honored me.

COUNT: I didn't recognize you. You are so big and stout . . .

FIGARO: What would you, my lord? it's hard times.

COUNT: Poor fellow! What are you doing in Seville? Not long ago I recommended you to a position in the government.

FIGARO: I received the appointment, my lord, and you have my gratitude.

COUNT: Call me Lindor. Don't you see by my disguise, that I want to be unknown?

FIGARO: I'll leave you.

COUNT: On the contrary. I await here the outcome of a certain matter, and two men chattering are not so suspicious as one alone pacing up and down. Let's appear to be chattering. Now, this position?

FIGARO: The minister, having considered Your Excellency's recommendation, had me appointed at once apothecary's boy.

COUNT: In the army hospitals?

FIGARO: No; in the Andalusian stud-farms.

COUNT: (*laughing*) A fine beginning!

FIGARO: The position wasn't a bad one, because, having dressings and drugs in my charge, I often sold men good horse medicines.

COUNT: Which killed the king's subjects!

FIGARO: Ha! Ha! There is no universal remedy that has not sometimes cured Galicians, Catalans, and Auvergnats.[2]

COUNT: Why, then, did you leave it?

FIGARO: Leave it? I was removed; someone maligned me to the powers. "Envy with crooked fingers, with mien pale and livid . . ."

COUNT: Oh! for pity's sake, my friend! Do you also make verses? I saw you scribbling away there on your knees and singing this very morning.

FIGARO: That is really the cause of my misfortune, Your Excellency. When they reported to the minister that I was making, I can tell you quite prettily, some garlands of verses to Chloris, that I was sending riddles to the newspapers, that madrigals done by me were the style; in a word, when he learned that I was everywhere in print, he took it tragically, and had me dismissed from my position on the pretext that a love of letters is incompatible with the spirit of business.

[2] *Galicia and Catalonia (principal city, Barcelona) are provinces of Spain. Auvergne is a province of France.*

COUNT: Powerfully reasoned! And you did not represent to him . . .

FIGARO: I believed myself only too happy to be forgotten by him, convinced that a grandee does us enough good when he does us no harm.

COUNT: You don't tell everything. I remember that in my service you were something of a rogue.

FIGARO: Good Heavens! my lord, it's because one wants the poor to be faultless.

COUNT: Lazy, wild . . .

FIGARO: In comparison with the virtues required of a servant, does Your Excellency know many masters worthy of being valets?

COUNT: (*laughing*) Not bad. And you withdrew to this city?

FIGARO: No, not immediately.

COUNT: (*stopping him*) One moment . . . I thought it was she . . . Keep on talking, I can hear you anyway.

FIGARO: On my return to Madrid, I was determined to try my literary talents again, and the theatre appeared to me a field of honor . . .

COUNT: Ah! God help us!

FIGARO: (*During his reply, the* COUNT *looks attentively in the direction of the blinds.*) In truth, I do not know how I did not have the greatest success, for I had filled the orchestra with the most excellent workers, with hands . . . like bats; I had prohibited gloves, canes, everything that produces only dull applause; and upon my honor, before the play was performed, the café appeared quite well disposed toward me, but the efforts of the cabal . . .

COUNT: Ah, the cabal! The last resort of a fallen author!

FIGARO: As well as anyone else: why not? They hissed me, but if I can get them together again . . .

COUNT: Boredom will certainly take your revenge against them?

FIGARO: Ah! how I have it in for them, indeed!

COUNT: You swear! Do you know that in the courthouse one has only twenty-four hours to curse one's judges?

FIGARO: One has twenty-four years in the theatre; life is too short to use up such resentment.

COUNT: Your joyous anger delights me. But you didn't tell me what made you leave Madrid.

FIGARO: My guardian angel, Your Excellency, since I am happy enough to find my old master again. Seeing that, at Madrid, the republic of letters is that of wolves, constantly at one another's throats, and that, delivered to the scorn which this ridiculous persistence leads them, all the insects, mosquitoes,[3] gnats, critics, all the envious, journalists, booksellers, censors, and all that can cling to the hide of the unfortunate men of letters, completed tearing to shreds and sucking the little substance they had left; weary of writing, bored with myself, disgusted with others, full of debts, and light in cash; finally, convinced that this tangible revenue from the razor is preferable to the empty honors of the pen,

[3] *Beaumarchais uses* moustiques *and* maringouins, *both of which mean "mosquitoes." One of the words is not translated.*

I left Madrid, and, my baggage upon my shoulder, philosophically crossing the two Castiles,[4] La Mancha, Estremadura, Sierra Morena, Andalusia, welcomed in one town, imprisoned in the next, and everywhere superior to events; coming to one's aid in good times, enduring the bad; making fun of fools, defying the wicked; laughing at my poverty and shaving everyone; you see me finally established in Seville and ready to serve again Your Excellency in all it may be pleased to order me.

COUNT: Who gave you so gay a philosophy?

FIGARO: The habit of misfortune. I always hasten to laugh at everything for fear that I may be obliged to weep. What are you continually watching over there?

COUNT: Let us escape.

FIGARO: Why?

COUNT: Come, you wretch! You will be my destruction. (They hide.)

SCENE 3

BARTHOLO, ROSINE

(The blinds of the second story open, and BARTHOLO and ROSINE appear at the window.)

4 Old and New Castile, La Mancha, Estremadura, and Andalusia are provinces in Spain; Sierra Morena is a mountain range, situated in the southwest part of Spain.

ROSINE: How pleasant it is to breathe the fresh air! These blinds are so rarely opened . . .

BARTHOLO: What paper are you holding in your hand?

ROSINE: They are some couplets from *The Useless Precaution*,[5] which my singing teacher gave me yesterday.

BARTHOLO: What is *The Useless Precaution?*

ROSINE: It's a new comedy.

BARTHOLO: Another play! A new sort of folly!

ROSINE: I know nothing about it.

BARTHOLO: Hm! hm! the newspapers and the authorities will give us satisfaction. Barbarous century . . . !

ROSINE: You're always insulting our poor century.

BARTHOLO: Pardon the liberty I'm taking: what has it produced to be worthy of praise? Silly things of all kinds: liberty of thought, gravitation, electricity, religious tolerance, inoculation, quinine, the *Encyclopédie*,[6] and plays.

ROSINE: (*as the paper drops from her hand and falls into the street*) Ah! my song! my song fell while I was listening to you; run, run, sir; my song! it will be lost.

BARTHOLO: Confound it! When one has it one holds it. (*He leaves the balcony.*)

ROSINE: (*looks inside the room and signals in the street*)

[5] La Précaution Inutile *is the subtitle of* Le Barbier de Séville. *See* Figaro's *last speech in the play.*

[6] *The* Encyclopédie, *published by Diderot and by D'Alembert, was the mouthpiece of the* philosophes, *who believed in the scientific determinism, derived from Bacon, Descartes, Locke, and Newton, and championed the skepticism and the rationalism of their century (the 18th). Its attacks on legal, social, and clerical abuses paved the way for the French Revolution.*

S't, s't, (*the* COUNT *appears*), pick it up quickly and effect an escape. (*The* COUNT *jumps only once, seizes the paper, and retreats.*)

BARTHOLO: (*leaves the home and searches*) Where is it? I don't see anything.

ROSINE: Under the balcony, at the foot of the wall.

BARTHOLO: You've given me a fine errand! Has someone passed by?

ROSINE: I haven't seen anyone.

BARTHOLO: (*aside*) And I who have been so good as to search . . . Bartholo, you are indeed a simpleton, my friend: this should teach you never to open blinds facing the street. (*He goes into the house.*)

ROSINE: (*still on the balcony*) My excuse lies in my unhappiness; alone, locked up, a prey to the persecution of an odious man, is it a crime to attempt to escape the bonds of slavery?

BARTHOLO: (*appearing on the balcony*) Go in, young lady;[7] it is my fault if you have lost your song, but this misfortune won't come to you again, I swear it. (*He locks up the blinds.*)

---

[7] *Bartholo often addresses Rosine as* Signora, *which is the usual Italian for "married lady," "Mrs."*

SCENE 4

THE COUNT, FIGARO

(*They enter warily.*)

COUNT: Now that they have gone in, let us examine this song, in which a mystery is surely enclosed. It's a note.

FIGARO: He asked what *The Useless Precaution* is.

COUNT: (*reads excitedly*) "Your devotion moves my curiosity; as soon as my guardian has gone out, sing unconcernedly to the well-known air of these couplets something which shall tell me the name, the rank, and the intention of the one who seems so obstinately attached to the unfortunate Rosine."

FIGARO: (*imitating Rosine's voice*) My song! my song has fallen; run, run quickly. (*He laughs.*) Ha! ha! ha! Oh! these women! Do you wish to give cunning to the most naïve? Just shut her up.

COUNT: My dear Rosine!

FIGARO: My lord, I am no longer anxious about the motives for your masquerade, you are making love in prospect.

COUNT: Now you know how it is, but if you chatter . . .

FIGARO: I, chatter! To reassure you I shall not use the grand phrases of honor and devotion which are nowadays abused. I have only one word to say; my self-interest answers for my loyalty; weigh everything in that balance, and . . .

COUNT: Very well. Know, then, that chance made me meet, at the Prado,[8] six months ago, a young lady of such beauty . . . You have just seen her! I have sought her in vain through all Madrid. It was only a few days ago that I discovered that her name is Rosine, that she is of noble blood, an orphan, and married to an old doctor of this city, who is called Bartholo.

FIGARO: A fine bird, indeed! a hard nut to crack! But who told you that she was the doctor's wife?

COUNT: Everyone.

FIGARO: It's a story made up by him on his arrival from Madrid, to give the slip to the gallants and put them off the scent. She is still only his ward, but soon . . .

COUNT: (sharply) Never. Ah! what news! I was resolved to dare everything to offer my regrets, and snatch her from the unworthy husband to whom she is destined. Do you know the guardian?

FIGARO: As well as I know my mother.

COUNT: What kind of a man is he?

FIGARO: (vivaciously) He is a handsome big, short, young old man, dapple gray, cunning, clean shaven, blasé, peeping and prying, grumbling and groaning, all at once.

COUNT: (grown impatient) Hey! I have seen him. And his character?

FIGARO: Brutal, stingy, in love, and jealous to excess of his ward, who hates him to death.

---

[8] The Prado is the national Spanish museum of painting and sculpture. It is in Madrid.

COUNT: So his means of pleasing are . . .

FIGARO: Zero.

COUNT: So much the better. His integrity?

FIGARO: Just enough not to be hanged.

COUNT: So much the better. To punish a scoundrel while I find my happiness . . .

FIGARO: Is to do at the same time a public and private good; really, a masterpiece of morality, my lord!

COUNT: You say that fear of gallants makes him keep his door closed upon her.

FIGARO: Upon everyone; if only he could stop it up.

COUNT: Ah! the devil! so much the worse. Do you happen to have access to his house?

FIGARO: Have I? First, the house I occupy belongs to the doctor, who lodges me there *gratis*.

COUNT: Ha! ha!

FIGARO: Yes, indeed. And I, as a sign of gratitude, promise him ten gold pistoles[9] a year, also *gratis*.

COUNT: (*impatiently*) You are his tenant?

FIGARO: Furthermore I'm his barber, his surgeon, his pharmacist; there isn't a razor, lancet or syringe stroke which does not come from the hand of your humble servant.

COUNT: (*embracing him*) Ah! Figaro, my friend, you will be my angel, my savior, my tutelary genius.

FIGARO: A plague take you! How readily has my useful-

[9] *The gold pistole is the old quarter doubloon of Spain, worth about four dollars.*

ness brought distances closer! Talk to me of people with a passion.

COUNT: Fortunate Figaro! you are going to see my Rosine! you are going to see her! Can you imagine your good fortune?

FIGARO: That's lover's talk, all right! Do I adore her? Would that you could take my place!

COUNT: Ah! if we could dodge the watchers! . . .

FIGARO: That's what I was thinking of.

COUNT: For only twelve hours!

FIGARO: By busying people with their own interests, one prevents their harming the interests of others.

COUNT: No doubt. Well?

FIGARO: (*thinking*) I'm racking my brains to see whether the pharmacy would not furnish a few little innocent means . . .

COUNT: Villain!

FIGARO: Do I want to harm them? They all need my service. It's only a matter of treating them all together.

COUNT: But this physician may grow suspicious.

FIGARO: We must work so quickly that he'll have no time to suspect. I have an idea. The regiment of the heir-apparent has just arrived in this city.

COUNT: The colonel is one of my friends.

FIGARO: Good. Go to the doctor in a horseman's uniform with your billet; he will have to lodge you, and I'll take care of the rest.

COUNT: Excellent!

FIGARO: It would be still better if you looked a little inebriated . . .

COUNT: What's the good?

FIGARO: And treat him a bit freely, so you have a fine excuse for being unreasonable.

COUNT: What's the good of that?

FIGARO: So that he may take no offense and believe you more in haste to sleep than carry on intrigues in his house.

COUNT: Superiorly planned! But why don't you go yourself?

FIGARO: Ah! I, indeed! We shall be quite fortunate if he does not recognize you. You, whom he has never seen. And how am I to introduce you afterward?

COUNT: You are right.

FIGARO: It is because perhaps you cannot act this difficult part. Horseman . . . a bit drunk . . .

COUNT: You're making fun of me! (*imitating the speech of a drunkard*) Isn't this the house of Doctor Bartholo, my friend?

FIGARO: Not bad, truly; only a bit more unsteady in the legs. (*In a more drunken voice.*) Isn't this the house . . .

COUNT: For shame! you have the drunkenness of the people.

FIGARO: It's the good one, the one of pleasure.

COUNT: The door opens.

FIGARO: It's our man. Let us go away until he has left.

SCENE 5

THE COUNT *and* FIGARO *hidden,* BARTHOLO

BARTHOLO: (*comes out, speaking to someone in the house*) I'll be back in an instant, let no one enter. How foolish of me to have come down! As soon as she begged me to, I should have suspected . . . And why is Bazile so late! He was to arrange everything for my secret marriage tomorrow; and no news! Let us go see what may have delayed him.

SCENE 6

THE COUNT, FIGARO

COUNT: What did I hear? Tomorrow he marries Rosine secretly!

FIGARO: My lord, the difficulty of success only adds to the necessity of undertaking.

COUNT: What kind of man is this Bazile who is meddling with the doctor's marriage?

FIGARO: A poor devil who teaches music to the doctor's ward, infatuated with his art, a bit of a scoundrel, needy, on his knees before a crown, and whom it will be easy to manage, my lord . . . (*gazing at the blinds*) There she is! there she is!

COUNT: Who?

FIGARO: Behind the blinds. There she is! there she is! Don't look, please don't look!

COUNT: Why?

FIGARO: Did she not write to you: *Sing unconcernedly?* That is to say, sing as if you were singing . . . only for the sake of singing. Oh! there she is! there she is!

COUNT: Since I have begun to interest her without being known to her, I shall not give up the name of Lindor which I have assumed, in fact, my triumph will have greater charms. (*He opens the paper that* ROSINE *has thrown out of the window.*) But how can I sing to this music? I cannot make verses.

FIGARO: Everything that will come to you, my lord, will be excellent; in love, the heart assists the productions of the mind . . . and take my guitar.

COUNT: What do you want me to do with it? I play so badly!

FIGARO: Can a man like you be ignorant of anything! with the back of the hand; tum, tum, tum . . . To sing without a guitar in Seville! you would soon be recognized, indeed, you would soon be tracked down. (FIGARO *sticks close to the wall under the balcony.*)

COUNT: (*sings, as he walks to and fro and accompanies himself on his guitar*)

FIRST COUPLET

Thou shalt know my name, for to command is thine,
More unknown, I dared to adore thee:
My name once known, what shall I hope?
What matters it? My master's will is mine.

FIGARO: (*in a low voice*) Fine, to be sure! Courage, my lord.

COUNT: SECOND COUPLET

I am Lindor, of common birth and nation,
A simple student's life is all I claim;
Alas! why have I not some brilliant knight's name
To offer thee his rank and his station.

FIGARO: Hey! what the dickens! I, who pique myself on my verses, could do no better.

COUNT: THIRD COUPLET

Every morning, here, with a tender voice,
I shall proclaim my hopeless love;
I shall bound my pleasures to seeing thee,
And mayest thou find some in listening to me!

FIGARO: Oh! indeed, this last one! . . . (*He approaches and kisses the hem of his master's cloak.*)

COUNT: Figaro?

FIGARO: Your Excellency?

COUNT: Do you think I have been heard!

ROSINE: (*within, sings*)

Air of the *Maître en droit*
All tells me that Lindor is charming,
That I must love him with constancy . . .

(*They hear a window closing noisily.*)

FIGARO: Do you think you have been heard this time?

COUNT: She has shut her window; someone has apparently entered the room.

FIGARO: Ah! the poor little thing, how she trembles as she sings! She is caught, my lord.

COUNT: She uses the same means she herself pointed out. *All tells me that Lindor is charming.* What grace! what wit!

FIGARO: What slyness! what love!

COUNT: Do you believe she will marry me, Figaro?

FIGARO: She will pass through these blinds rather than fail to do so.

COUNT: It's all over, I am Rosine's . . . forever.

FIGARO: You forget, my lord, that she can no longer hear you.

COUNT: Master Figaro, I have but one word to say to you: she will be my wife; and if you further my plan by hiding my true name from her . . . you understand me, you know me . . .

FIGARO: I surrender. Come, Figaro, your fortune is made, my boy.

COUNT: Let us withdraw, for fear of arousing suspicion.

FIGARO: (*in lively fashion*) I'll enter this home, where, by the strength of my wit, I am going with a single stroke of a wand, put vigilance to sleep, awake love, mislead jealousy, misguide intrigue, and overcome all obstacles.

You, my lord, my house, the soldier's uniform, the billet, and gold in your pockets.

COUNT: Gold, for whom?

FIGARO: (*impatiently*) Gold, for Heaven's sake! gold, it is the sinews of intrigue.[10]

COUNT: Don't get angry, Figaro, I shall bring a good deal of it.

FIGARO: (*going away*) I shall rejoin you presently.

COUNT: Figaro?

FIGARO: What is it?

COUNT: Your guitar?

FIGARO: (*comes back*) I have forgotten my guitar! I must be insane! (*Exit.*)

COUNT: And your house, stupid?

FIGARO: (*comes back*) Ah! really I am panicky! My shop, a few steps away, painted blue, with leaden windows, three paddles in the air, an eye in the hand, with a motto: *Consilio manuque,*[11] FIGARO. (*He runs away.*)

---

[10] *Perhaps an imitation of Machiavelli,* Discorsi sopra la prima Deca di Tito Livio, II, 10: *"I danari non sono il nervo della guerra, secondo che è la comune opinione." There is a common proverb: "Money is the sinews of war."*

[11] *In Latin this means: "With advice and hand."*

ACT TWO

The stage represents the apartment of Rosine. The window at the rear of the stage is closed by a barred shutter.

SCENE I

ROSINE: (*alone, a candlestick in her hand, she takes some paper from the table and begins to write*) Marceline is sick, all the servants are busy, and no one sees me write. I do not know whether these walls have eyes or ears, or whether my Argus[1] has an evil genius who informs him in the nick of time, but I cannot say one word or take one step whose purpose he does not immediately guess . . . Ah! Lindor! . . . (*She reads the letter.*) I must seal my letter, although I do not know when or how I may deliver it to him. I saw him, through my blinds, talking for a long time to the barber Figaro. He's a good man who has sometimes shown me pity; if I could only speak with him for a moment.

[1] *Argus or Argos, according to mythology, had a hundred eyes. The allusion is clearly to Bartholo.*

SCENE 2

ROSINE, FIGARO

ROSINE: (*surprised*) Ah! Master Figaro, how glad I am to see you!

FIGARO: Your health, madam?

ROSINE: Not too good, Master Figaro. I am dying of boredom.

FIGARO: I believe it; it fattens only fools.

ROSINE: With whom were you talking so earnestly down there? I did not hear, but . . .

FIGARO: With a young student, a relative of mine, a young man of great promise, full of wit, sentiment, and talent, and moreover, with a most attractive face.

ROSINE: Ah! very fine, I assure you! What's his name? . . .

FIGARO: Lindor. He has nothing. But, if he had not left Madrid in such a hurry, he could have found some good position there.

ROSINE: He will find one, Master Figaro, he will find one. A young man such as you portray him is not born to remain unknown.

FIGARO: (*aside*) Very well. (*aloud*) But he has one great fault which will always harm his advancement.

ROSINE: A fault, Master Figaro! A fault! are you quite sure?

FIGARO: He is in love.

ROSINE: He is in love! and you call that a fault?

FIGARO: Truly, it is one only in regard to his poor fortune.

ROSINE: Ah! how unjust is fate! And does he name the person he loves? I am so curious . . .

FIGARO: You are the last one, madam,[2] to whom I would entrust such a secret as this.

ROSINE: (*with animation*) Why, Master Figaro? I am discreet; this young man is your relative, he interests me greatly . . . Tell me, then . . .

FIGARO: (*gazing at her slyly*) Imagine the prettiest little darling, sweet, tender, trim, and fresh, kindling one's appetite, with a dainty foot, a figure neat and slender, plump arms, a rosy mouth, and hands! cheeks! teeth! eyes! . . .

ROSINE: Who lives in this city?

FIGARO: In this quarter.

ROSINE: On this street, perhaps?

FIGARO: But two steps from me.

ROSINE: Ah, how charming it is! . . . for your relative. And this person is? . . .

FIGARO: I have not named her?

ROSINE: (*animatedly*) It is the only thing you have forgotten, Master Figaro. Please tell me, please tell me quickly; if someone should enter, I could no longer know . . .

[2] *In French classical tragedy and comedy, young unmarried ladies are addressed as* madame. *This is the case with Corneille, Racine, Molière, and Voltaire.*

FIGARO: Do you want to know absolutely, madam? Well, this person is . . . your guardian's ward.

ROSINE: Ward? . . .

FIGARO: Doctor Bartholo's, yes, madam.

ROSINE: (*with emotion*) Ah! Master Figaro! . . . I do not believe you, I assure you.

FIGARO: And that is what he is longing to come and convince you of himself.

ROSINE: You make me tremble, Master Figaro.

FIGARO: For shame, tremble! a bad reckoning, madam; when one yields to the fears of evil, one feels already the evil of fear. Moreover, I have just rid you of all your watchers till tomorrow.

ROSINE: If he loves me, he must prove it to me by remaining absolutely quiet.

FIGARO: Hey! madam, can love and rest dwell in the same heart? Poor youth is so unhappy nowadays that it has only this terrible choice: love without rest, or rest without love.

ROSINE: (*lowering her eyes*) Rest without love . . . appears . . .

FIGARO: Ah! very languid. It seems, in fact, that love without rest cuts a better figure; and, as for me, if I were a woman . . .

ROSINE: (*in embarrassment*) It is certain that a young lady cannot prevent a gentleman from esteeming her; but, if he were to do something imprudent, Master Figaro, he would ruin us.

FIGARO: (*aside*) He would ruin us! (*aloud*) If you would prohibit expressly in a little letter . . . A letter has a good deal of power.

ROSINE: (*gives him the letter which she has just written*) I have not the time to begin this over again, but when you give it to him, tell him . . . well, tell him . . . (*She listens.*)

FIGARO: Nobody, madam.

ROSINE: That all I do is out of pure friendship.

FIGARO: That goes without saying. Zounds! love surely has a different pace!

ROSINE: Only out of pure friendship, do you understand? All I fear is that, disheartened by difficulties . . .

FIGARO: Yes, some will-o'-the-wisp. Remember, madam, that the wind that blows out a light kindles a brazier, and that we are that brazier. Talking of it only, he exhales such a flame that he has almost animated me with his passion, I who have nothing to do with the matter.

ROSINE: Dear me! I hear my guardian. If he should find you here . . . Go out through the harpsichord-room, and go down as softly as you can.

FIGARO: Be quiet about it. (*aside*) This is worth more than my observations. (*He goes into the harpsichord-room.*)

SCENE 3

ROSINE: (*alone*) I am dying of worry until he is outside. How I like him, that good Figaro! He is quite an honest fellow, a good relative. Ah! there is my tyrant; let me take up my work again. (*She blows out the candle, sits down, takes up an embroidery frame.*)

SCENE 4

BARTHOLO, ROSINE

BARTHOLO: (*angry*) Ah, curses upon that madman, that piratical scoundrel of Figaro! there now, can one leave one's house one moment, and be sure when one comes back . . .

ROSINE: Who puts you in such a rage, sir?

BARTHOLO: That confounded barber who has just crippled my whole household in one fell swoop. He has given L'Éveillé an opiate, La Jeunesse, a sneezing powder; he has bled Marceline in her foot; even down to my mule . . . He has put a poultice on the eyes of a poor blind beast! because he owed me a hundred crowns, he is in haste to balance his account. Ah! let him bring them! And nobody in the anteroom, one could enter this apartment as easily as the parade-ground.

ROSINE: And who can enter it but you, sir?

BARTHOLO: I prefer to fear unreasonably to exposing myself without precaution. There are enterprising, daring people everywhere . . . This very morning, did not someone quickly pick up your song while I was going down to look for it? Oh! I . . .

ROSINE: This is surely giving importance to everything just for the pleasure of it! The wind can have carried the paper off, the first passer-by, what-not?

BARTHOLO: The wind, the first passer-by! . . . There is no wind, madam, there is no first passer-by in the world: there is always someone set there on purpose to pick up all the papers that a woman affects to drop inadvertently.

ROSINE: Affects, sir?

BARTHOLO: Yes, madam, affects.

ROSINE: (*aside*) Oh! the wicked old man!

BARTHOLO: But all that will not happen again, for I am going to have those bars sealed.

ROSINE: Do better than that; wall up all the windows at once. Between a prison and a dungeon the difference is so little.

BARTHOLO: As for those which look out upon the street, maybe it would not be so bad an idea . . . At least, that barber has not yet entered your apartment?

ROSINE: Is he also an object of worry?

BARTHOLO: As much as another.

ROSINE: How honest your replies are!

BARTHOLO: Ah! trust everybody, and you will soon have

in your house a good wife to deceive you, good friends to take her away from you, and good servants to help them do so.

ROSINE: What! you will not even concede that one has principles against the seduction of Master Figaro?

BARTHOLO: Who the deuce knows anything about the whimsicalness of woman?

ROSINE: (*angry*) But, sir, if it is enough to be a man to please us, why is it, then, that I dislike you so?

BARTHOLO: (*amazed*) Why? . . . why? . . . You do not answer my question about that barber?

ROSINE: (*beside herself*) Well, yes, that man came into my room, I saw him, I spoke to him. I shall not even hide from you that I found him quite pleasant; and may you die of chagrin! (*She goes out.*)

SCENE 5

BARTHOLO: (*alone*) Oh! those scoundrels! those dogs of servants! La Jeunesse! L'Éveillé! that cursed Éveillé!

SCENE 6

BARTHOLO, L'ÉVEILLÉ

L'ÉVEILLÉ: (*enters yawning, half asleep*) Aah! aah! ah! ah!

BARTHOLO: Where were you, confounded scatterbrain, when that barber entered here?

L'ÉVEILLÉ: Sir, I was . . . ah, aah, ah . . .

BARTHOLO: Hatching some prank, no doubt? And you did not see him?

L'ÉVEILLÉ: Surely I saw him, since he found me quite ill, as he said; and it must be true, for I began to have pains[3] in all my limbs, just hearing him talk[4] . . . Ah, ah, ah . . .

BARTHOLO: (*mimics him*) Just hearing him! . . . Where is that good-for-nothing La Jeunesse? To drug this little chap without my prescription! There is some knavery in it.

SCENE 7

THE PRECEDING ACTORS

(LA JEUNESSE *arrives as an old man, leaning upon a cane; he sneezes several times.*)

L'ÉVEILLÉ: (*still yawning*) La Jeunesse!

BARTHOLO: You will sneeze Sunday.

LA JEUNESSE: That's more than fifty . . . fifty times . . . in one minute. (*He sneezes*) I am aching all over.

BARTHOLO: What! I ask both of you whether someone

---

[3] Me douloir *is Old French. It is no longer used in Modern French.*
[4] *Only* parl . . . *is given because of his yawning. The rest of* parler *is understood.*

entered Rosine's apartment, and you do not tell me that that barber . . .

L'ÉVEILLÉ: (*continuing to yawn*) So Master Figaro is someone? Aah, ah . . .

BARTHOLO: I wager that the sly fellow has an understanding with him.

L'ÉVEILLÉ: (*weeping foolishly*) I, . . . I have an understanding! . . .

LA JEUNESSE: (*sneezing*) But, sir, is there . . . is there any justice?

BARTHOLO: Justice! Justice is good for you wretches! I am your master, I who am always right.

LA JEUNESSE: (*sneezing*) Why, of course, when a thing is true . . .

BARTHOLO: When a thing is true! If I do not want it to be true, I certainly contend that it is not true. If you would allow all those cads to be right, you would soon see what would become of authority.

LA JEUNESSE: (*sneezing*) I may as well hand in my resignation. It's a terrible position and always a devilish row.

L'ÉVEILLÉ: (*weeping*) A poor respectable man is treated like a wretch.

BARTHOLO: Go out, you poor respectable man. (*He mimics them.*) And t'chew and t'cha; one sneezes and the other yawns in my face.

LA JEUNESSE: Ah! sir, I swear that without Miss Rosine,

there would be . . . there would be no way of staying on in this house. (*He goes out sneezing.*)

SCENE 8

BARTHOLO, DON BAZILE; FIGARO, *hidden in the harpsichord-room, appears from time to time and listens to them*

BARTHOLO: Ah! Don Bazile, you have come to give Rosine her music lesson?

BAZILE: That is the least urgent.

BARTHOLO: I went to see you without finding you.

BAZILE: I had gone out on your business. You must learn some trying news.

BARTHOLO: For you?

BAZILE: No, for you. Count Almaviva is in this city.

BARTHOLO: Speak low. The one who had Rosine sought throughout all Madrid?

BAZILE: He is lodging in the Plaza and comes out every day incognito.

BARTHOLO: That concerns me, there is no doubt about it. And what shall I do?

BAZILE: If he were a private citizen, one would succeed in getting him out of the way.

BARTHOLO: Yes, we could ambush him one evening, armed with sword and breastplate.

BAZILE: *Bone Deus!* and thus compromise ourselves! To raise up a nasty business, all well and good, and meanwhile slander him according to the experts; *concedo.*[5]

BARTHOLO: That is an odd way of getting rid of a man!

BAZILE: Slander, sir? You hardly know what you scorn. I have seen the best of people nearly crushed under it. Believe me that there is no commonplace wickedness, no horror, no absurd tale, that one cannot make the idler of a large city adopt if one goes about it in the right way; and we have here some very skillful people! . . . First, a light rumor, skimming the ground like a swallow before the storm, *pianissimo,*[6] it murmurs and makes off, and sows its poisonous arrow as it flees. So-and-so picks it up, and *piano, piano* slips it gracefully into your ear. The evil is done, it sprouts, creeps, travels on, and *rinforzando* from mouth to mouth it goes at a dickens of a pace; then, all of a sudden, I do not know how, you see slander rising, hissing, swelling, visibly growing; it leaps forward, extends its flight, whirls, envelops, tears, drags, bursts, and thunders, and becomes, thanks to Heaven, a general cry, a public *crescendo,* a universal chorus of hatred and tabooing. Who the dickens could resist it?

BARTHOLO: What nonsense are you telling me, Bazile?

[5] Bone Deus *is the Latin vocative of* Bonus Deus; concedo *means in Latin "I grant, I concede."*

[6] *The terms used by Don Bazile are musical:* pianissimo *and* piano, piano *"very softly" are practically synonyms;* rinforzando *means "reënforcing";* crescendo *means "increasing." These Italian musical terms are used in English.*

And what connection can this *piano-crescendo* have with my situation?

BAZILE: What, what connection? What one does everywhere to put one's enemy out of the way must be done here to prevent yours approaching.

BARTHOLO: Approaching! I certainly intend to marry Rosine before she learns that this count even exists.

BAZILE: In that case, you have not a moment to lose.

BARTHOLO: And who is responsible, Bazile? I have entrusted all the details of this matter to you.

BAZILE: Yes. But you skimped on the expenses, and, in the harmony of good order, an unequal marriage, a wicked judgment, an evident injustice, are discords that should always be prepared for and prevented by the perfect accord of gold.

BARTHOLO: (*giving him money*) I see I must give in to you; but let's continue.

BAZILE: That's what is called talking. Tomorrow everything will be over; it's up to you to prevent anyone from informing your ward today.

BARTHOLO: Trust me. Are you coming this evening, Bazile?

BAZILE: Do not count on it. Your marriage alone will keep me busy all day. Do not count on it.

BARTHOLO: (*accompanies him*) Your servant.

BAZILE: Remain, doctor, please remain.

BARTHOLO: No. I want to close the street door after you.

SCENE 9

FIGARO: (*alone, coming out of the harpsichord-room*) Oh! a good precaution! Close, close your street door, and I am going to open it again to the count as I go out. That Bazile is a great villain, fortunately he is even more foolish. One must have a station, a family, a name, a rank, standing in short, to create a sensation in the world as a slanderer. But a Bazile! If he slandered, one would not believe him.

SCENE 10

ROSINE, *hastening*; FIGARO

ROSINE: What! you are still there, Master Figaro?

FIGARO: Very fortunately for you, miss. Your guardian and your singing teacher, believing themselves alone here, have just spoken openly . . .

ROSINE: And you listened to them, Master Figaro? But do you know that it is very wrong?

FIGARO: To listen? It is, however, the best way to hear well. Know that your guardian is preparing to marry you tomorrow.

ROSINE: Ah! good Heavens!

FIGARO: Do not fear anything; we shall give him so much work to do that he will not have time to think of it.

ROSINE: Here he comes back, please go out by the little staircase; you terrify me. (*Figaro runs away.*)

SCENE II

BARTHOLO, ROSINE

ROSINE: You were here with someone, sir?

BARTHOLO: Don Bazile, whom I have accompanied to the door, and with good reason. You would have liked it better that it had been Master Figaro.

ROSINE: That's all the same to me, I assure you.

BARTHOLO: I should certainly like to know what that barber was in such a hurry to tell you.

ROSINE: Must we speak seriously? He gave me an account of Marceline's condition, and she is not too well, so he says.

BARTHOLO: Give you an account? I shall wager that he was instructed to hand you some letter.

ROSINE: And from whom, if you please?

BARTHOLO: Oh, from whom! From someone whom women never name. How should I know? Perhaps the reply to the paper of the window.

ROSINE: (*aside*) He hasn't missed a single thing. (*aloud*) It would serve you right if it were.

BARTHOLO: (*looks at the hands of Rosine*) That is it. You have been writing.

ROSINE: (*in embarrassment*) It would be amusing indeed, if you made me acknowledge it.

BARTHOLO: (*taking her right hand*) I, not at all; but your finger still stained with ink! what of that, sly miss?

ROSINE: (*aside*) Cursed man!

BARTHOLO: (*still holding her hand*) A woman always thinks herself quite safe because she is alone.

ROSINE: Ah! no doubt . . . A fine proof! Please stop, sir, you are twisting my arm. I burned myself in playing with the candle, and I have always been told that you must dip it immediately in ink; that is what I did.

BARTHOLO: That is what you did? Let us see whether a second witness will corroborate the deposition of the first. I am certain that there were six sheets in this package of paper; for I count them every morning, even today.

ROSINE: (*aside*) Oh! what a fool! (*aloud*) The sixth.

BARTHOLO: (*counting*) Three, four, five; I see clearly there is no sixth.

ROSINE: (*dropping her eyes*) I used the sixth to make a bag for some bonbons which I sent to little Miss Figaro.

BARTHOLO: Little Miss Figaro? And the pen, which was brand new, how did it become black? Was it in writing little Miss Figaro's address?

ROSINE: (*aside*) This man has a genius for jealousy! . . . (*aloud*) It served me in retracing a faded flower in the jacket which I am embroidering for you.

BARTHOLO: How edifying that is! In order to be believed, my child, you should not blush when hiding the truth so rapidly; but that's what you do not know yet.

ROSINE: And who would not blush, sir, to see you draw such malignant inferences from the most innocent deeds?

BARTHOLO: Of course, I am wrong: to burn one's finger, to dip it in ink, to make bonbon bags for little Miss Figaro, and to design my jacket on an embroidery frame! what more innocent! But how many lies piled up to conceal a simple fact! . . . *I am alone, I am not seen; I may lie at my ease;* but the tip of the finger remains black! the pen is soiled, the paper is missing: one could not think of everything. Indeed, young lady, when I go into town, a good double lock shall be the answer for you.

SCENE 12

THE COUNT, BARTHOLO, ROSINE

COUNT: (*in a cavalry uniform, appearing to be tipsy and singing*) Let us wake her, etc.

BARTHOLO: What does this man want of us? A soldier! Go into your room, young lady.

COUNT: (*sings*) Let us wake her, (*and advances toward Rosine*) Which of you two, Mesdames, is called Doctor Balordo?[7] (*To* ROSINE, *in a low voice.*) I am Lindor.

[7] Balordo *is an Italian word meaning "dull." It gave the French word* balourd, *"awkward."*

BARTHOLO: Bartholo!

ROSINE: (*aside*) He speaks of Lindor.

COUNT: Balordo, Barque à l'eau, I don't care which.[8] It is only a question of knowing which of the two . . . (*To* ROSINE, *showing her a paper.*) Take this letter.

BARTHOLO: Which![9] you see very well that it is I. Which! Retire to your room, Rosine, this man appears to be tipsy.

ROSINE: That is why I am staying, sir; you are alone. A woman sometimes inspires a little respect.

BARTHOLO: Retire, retire; I am not timid.

SCENE 13

THE COUNT, BARTHOLO

COUNT: Oh! I recognized you by your description.

BARTHOLO: (*to the* COUNT, *who is clasping the letter*) What are you concealing in your pocket?

COUNT: I am concealing it in my pocket so that you may not know what it is.

BARTHOLO: My description? Those people are forever believing that they are talking to soldiers!

COUNT: Do you think that it is such a hard matter to make your portrait?

---

[8] *One must make a gesture when one says "je m'en moque comme de ça."*

[9] *The French feminine* Laquelle *is clearer.*

The shaky head, the bald crown,
Bleary eyes, the savage frown,
The fierce air of an Algonquin . . .

BARTHOLO: What does that mean? Are you here to insult me? Clear out at once.

COUNT: Clear out! Ah, for shame! that's bad talk! Can you read, doctor . . . Barbe à l'eau?

BARTHOLO: Another absurd question.

COUNT: Ah! don't let that worry you, for I who am at least as much of a doctor as you . . .

BARTHOLO: How is that?

COUNT: Am I not horse-doctor for the regiment? That is why they have billeted me on purpose with a colleague.

BARTHOLO: To dare compare a farrier! . . .

COUNT: AIR: *Vive le vin*

Without singing.	No, doctor, I do not claim That our art can put to shame Hippocrates and his crew.
Singing.	Your knowledge, comrade, 'tis true, Has a success of a wider sway: For, if the ill its bears not away At least it bears off the patient.

Isn't what I am saying polite?

BARTHOLO: It becomes you well, ignorant manipulator, to debase thus the first, the greatest, and the most useful of arts.

COUNT: Completely useful for those who practice it.

BARTHOLO: An art whose successes the sun does honor to shine upon.

COUNT: And whose blunders the earth is anxious to cover.

BARTHOLO: I see very well, you lout, that you are accustomed to speaking only to horses.

COUNT: Speak to horses! Ah! Doctor, for a witty doctor . . . Isn't it notorious that the farrier always cures his patients without talking; whereas the physician talks a lot to his . . .

BARTHOLO: Without curing them, you mean?

COUNT: It's you who have said it.

BARTHOLO: Who the deuce sends this cursed drunkard here?

COUNT: I believe you are firing love-epigrams at me!

BARTHOLO: Well, what do you want? What do you ask?

COUNT: (*pretending a great anger*) Well, then he flares up. What do I want? Don't you see?

SCENE 14

ROSINE, THE COUNT, BARTHOLO

ROSINE: (*hastening*) Master soldier, don't flare up, please. (*To* BARTHOLO) Speak to him gently, sir; an unreasonable man.

COUNT: You are right; *he* is unreasonable, but *we* are reasonable! I, polite, and you, pretty . . . In fact, that's enough. The truth is I want to have dealings with no one in the house but you.

ROSINE: What can I do for you, sir?

COUNT: A mere trifle, my child. But if there is any obscure meaning in my sentences . . .

ROSINE: I'll catch their spirit.

COUNT: (*showing her the letter*) No, stick to the letter, the letter. It's only this . . . but I tell you with all respect, all honor, that you give me a bed tonight.

BARTHOLO: Is that all?

COUNT: No more. Read the billet doux that our quartermaster sergeant has written you.

BARTHOLO: Let us see. (*The* COUNT *hides the letter and gives him another paper.* BARTHOLO *reads*) "Doctor Bartholo will receive, feed, lodge, bed . . ."

COUNT: (*laying stress*) Bed.

BARTHOLO: "For one night only, one called Lindor the Scholar, horseman in the regiment . . ."

ROSINE: It is he, it is he himself.

BARTHOLO: (*fast, to* ROSINE) What's the matter?

COUNT: Well, am I wrong now, Doctor Barbaro?

BARTHOLO: One would think that this man derives a malicious pleasure in crippling me in every possible way. A plague take you! Barbaro! Barbe à l'eau! and tell your impertinent quartermaster sergeant that since my journey to Madrid I am exempt from billeting soldiers.

COUNT: (*aside*) Oh Heaven! What a troublesome mishap!

BARTHOLO: Ha! ha! our friend, that vexes you and sobers you up a little? But clear out, nonetheless, at once.

COUNT: (*aside*) I almost betrayed myself! (*aloud*) Clear out! If you are exempt from soldiers, you are not exempt from politeness, possibly? Clear out! Show me your exemption warrant; although, I cannot read, I'll soon see . . .

BARTHOLO: That shall be no obstacle. It is in this bureau.

COUNT: (*while* BARTHOLO *goes, says without moving*) Ah! my fair Rosine!

ROSINE: What! Lindor, is it you?

COUNT: In any case, take this letter.

ROSINE: Take care, he has his eyes on us.

COUNT: Take out your handkerchief, I'll drop the letter. (*He approaches.*)

BARTHOLO: Gently, gently, master soldier, I do not like my wife being looked at so closely.

COUNT: She is your wife?

BARTHOLO: Well! what then?

COUNT: I took you for her grandfather, paternal, maternal, sempiternal; there are at least three generations between her and you.

BARTHOLO: (*reads a parchment*) "In consideration of good and faithful testimony offered us . . .

COUNT: (*strikes the parchments with his hand so that they land on the floor*) Do I need all this verbiage?

BARTHOLO: Do you know, soldier, that if I call my people, I'll have you treated at once as you deserve.

COUNT: A fight! Ah! gladly. A fight! that is my trade. (*showing his belt pistol*) And here is something to throw powder into their eyes. You perhaps have never seen a battle, madam?

ROSINE: Nor do I want to see one.

COUNT: Nothing, however, is so gay as a battle. Imagine (*pushing the doctor*) at first that the enemy is on one side of the ravine, and the friends on the other. (*To* ROSINE, *showing her the letter*) Take out your handkerchief. (*He spits on the floor*) That's the ravine, that's understood. (ROSINE *draws her handkerchief, the* COUNT *drops his letter between them.*)

BARTHOLO: (*stooping*) Ha! ha!

COUNT: (*takes the letter and says*) Here it is . . . I who was going to teach you all the secrets of my trade . . . In truth, a very discreet lady! Has she not just dropped a billet doux from her pocket?

BARTHOLO: Give it to me, give it to me.

COUNT: *Dulciter,*[10] papa! each one his business. If a prescription of rhubarb had fallen from yours . . .

ROSINE: (*reaches for it*) Ah! I know what it is, master soldier. (*She takes the letter, which she hides in the little pocket of her apron.*)

BARTHOLO: Are you going to get out?

COUNT: Well, I'll go; goodbye, doctor; no bitterness. A little compliment, my dear man: pray death to forget me

[10] Dulciter *is the Latin for "agreeably, sweetly."*

for a few more campaigns; life has never been so dear to me.

BARTHOLO: Please go, if I had that influence with death . . .

COUNT: With death. Ah! doctor, you do so much for her that she has nothing to refuse you. (*Exit.*)

SCENE 15

BARTHOLO, ROSINE

BARTHOLO: (*looks at him go*) He has left at last. (*aside*) Let us dissimulate.

ROSINE: Confess, however, sir, that he is very lively, that young soldier! in spite of his drunkenness, one can see that he lacks neither wit nor a certain breeding.

BARTHOLO: Luckily, my love, we were able to get rid of him! Aren't you a bit curious to read with me the paper which he handed you?

ROSINE: What paper?

BARTHOLO: The one that he pretended to pick up to make you accept it.

ROSINE: All right! that is the letter from my cousin, the officer, which had dropped from my pocket.

BARTHOLO: I have an idea that he drew it from his own.

ROSINE: I recognized it very easily.

BARTHOLO: What does it cost to look at it?

ROSINE: I do not know what I have done with it.

BARTHOLO: (*pointing to her little pocket*) You put it there.

ROSINE: Ah! ah! absent-mindedly.

BARTHOLO: Ah! surely. You are going to see that it is probably some piece of foolishness.

ROSINE: (*aside*) There is no way of refusing him unless I make him angry.

BARTHOLO: Please give it to me, my dear.

ROSINE: But what do you mean by insisting, sir? Do you distrust me?

BARTHOLO: But you, what reason have you not to show it?

ROSINE: I repeat, sir, that this paper is no other than the letter from my cousin, which you gave me back yesterday unsealed; and, since this is the question, I shall tell you frankly, that this liberty of yours displeases me exceedingly.

BARTHOLO: I do not understand you!

ROSINE: Am I going to examine the papers addressed to you? Why do you take it upon yourself to touch those that are addressed to me? If it is jealousy, it insults me; if it comes to the abuse of a usurped authority, I am even more indignant.

BARTHOLO: What, indignant! You have never spoken to me thus.

ROSINE: If I have been moderate up to this day, it was not to give you the right to offend me with impunity.

BARTHOLO: Of what offense do you speak?

ROSINE: It's because it is unheard of for one to allow oneself to open others' letters.

BARTHOLO: One's wife?

ROSINE: I am not yet your wife. But why should she be made the object of an indignity that is not imposed upon anyone?

BARTHOLO: You want to deceive me and divert my attention from the note, which is, no doubt, a missive from some lover! but I shall see it, I assure you.

ROSINE: You shall not see it. If you come close to me, I'll flee from this house and I'll ask refuge of the first one who comes along.

BARTHOLO: Who will not receive you.

ROSINE: We shall see about that.

BARTHOLO: Here we are not in France, where one always agrees with women; but in order to destroy your whim, I am going to lock the door.

ROSINE: (*while he leaves to do so*) Ah Heaven! What shall I do? . . . Let us put quickly in its place my cousin's letter, and give him a chance to find it. (*She makes the exchange and puts her cousin's letter in the little pocket, so that it protrudes a little.*)

BARTHOLO: (*coming back*) Ah! now I hope to see it.

ROSINE: By what right, if you please?

BARTHOLO: By the right most universally recognized, that of the stronger.

ROSINE: You will have to kill me rather than get it from me.

BARTHOLO: (*stamping his foot*) Madam! Madam!

ROSINE: (*falling into an armchair, pretends that she is ill*) Ah! what an outrage! . . .

BARTHOLO: Give me that letter, or fear my anger.

ROSINE: (*falls backwards*) Unhappy Rosine!

BARTHOLO: What is wrong with you?

ROSINE: What a frightful future!

BARTHOLO: Rosine!

ROSINE: I am choking with rage!

BARTHOLO: She is ill.

ROSINE: I am growing weaker, I am dying.

BARTHOLO: (*aside*) Heavens! the letter! Let us read it without her knowing it. (*He feels her pulse and takes the letter, which he attempts to read by turning aside a bit.*)

ROSINE: (*still reclining*) Unfortunate one! ah!

BARTHOLO: (*drops her arm and says aside*) How mad is one to learn what one always fears to learn.

ROSINE: Ah! poor Rosine!

BARTHOLO: The use of perfumes . . . produces these spasmodic affections. (*He reads behind the armchair while he feels her pulse. ROSINE rises a little, looks at him slyly, makes a gesture with her head, and falls back without a word.*)

BARTHOLO: (*aside*) O Heaven! it is her cousin's letter. Cursed concern! How shall I appease her now? At least, let her not know that I have read it. (*He makes believe he raises her up and slips the letter back into her little pocket.*)

ROSINE: (*sighs*) Ah! . . .

BARTHOLO: Well! it is nothing, my child; a little attack of the vapors, that is all: for your pulse has not varied a bit. (*He turns to take a flask from the console-table.*)

ROSINE: (*aside*) He has replaced my letter: very well!

BARTHOLO: My dear Rosine, a little of these spirits.

ROSINE: I want nothing from you; leave me.

BARTHOLO: I admit that I was too rough about the note.

ROSINE: It is quite a different matter from the note. It is your manner of asking for things which is revolting.

BARTHOLO: (*on his knees*) I beg your pardon; I soon saw that I was quite wrong, and you see me at your feet, ready to make amends.

ROSINE: Yes, pardon! When you believe that this letter does not come from my cousin.

BARTHOLO: Whether it comes from someone else or from him, I do not want any explanation.

ROSINE: (*offering him the letter*) You see that with good behavior one obtains everything of me. Read it.

BARTHOLO: This open manner would dissipate my suspicions if I were unfortunate enough to keep some.

ROSINE: Please read it, sir.

BARTHOLO: (*draws back*) God forbid that I should so wrong you!

ROSINE: You will put me out by refusing it.

BARTHOLO: Receive as amends this token of my most perfect confidence. I am going to see poor Marceline, whom that Figaro has, I know not why, bled in the foot; aren't you coming, too?

ROSINE: I shall come up in a moment.

BARTHOLO: Since peace has been made, my darling, give me your hand. If you could only love me! ah! how happy you would be!

ROSINE: (*dropping her eyes*) If you could only please me, ah! how I should love you!

BARTHOLO: I will please you, I will please you; when I tell you that I will please you! (*Exit.*)

SCENE 16

ROSINE: (*watches him leave*) Ah! Lindor! He says he will please me! . . . Let us read this letter, which came near causing me so much sorrow. (*She reads and exclaims.*) Ah! . . . I have read too late: he enjoins me to keep an open quarrel with my guardian; I had a good opportunity, and I let it slip by. When I received this letter, I felt that I was blushing to the eyes. Ah! my guardian is right. I am quite far from having that experience with the world which, he often tells me, assures the control of women on every occasion; but an unjust man would succeed in making a slyboots of innocence itself.

ACT THREE

SCENE 1

BARTHOLO: (*alone and grieving*) What whims! what whims! She appeared appeased . . . There, let someone tell me who the dickens has stuck into her head not to take any more lessons from Don Bazile! She knows that he has something to do with my marriage . . . (*Someone knocks at the door*) Do everything in the world to please women; if you omit a single little point . . . I say one only . . . (*Someone knocks a second time*) Let's see who it is.

SCENE 2

BARTHOLO, THE COUNT, *as a student*

COUNT: May peace and joy ever dwell herein!

BARTHOLO: (*curtly*) Never was wish more opportune. What do you want?

COUNT: Sir, I am Alonzo, bachelor, *licencié*[1] . . .

BARTHOLO: I have no need of a tutor.

COUNT: . . . The pupil of Don Bazile, organist to the

[1] *In Spain a* licencié (*Span.* licenciado) *is someone who has obtained a university degree.*

Grand Convent, who has the honor to teach music to madam, your . . .

BARTHOLO: Bazile! organist! who has the honor! I know it, come to the point.

COUNT: (*aside*) What a man! (*aloud*) A sudden illness which forces him to keep to his bed . . .

BARTHOLO: Keep to his bed! Bazile! He has done well to send me word; I am going to see him at once.

COUNT: (*aside*) Ah, the devil! (*aloud*) When I say his bed, sir, I . . . I mean his room.

BARTHOLO: Were it only a trifling thing, go ahead, I'll follow you.

COUNT: (*embarrassed*) Sir, I was commissioned . . . Nobody can hear us?

BARTHOLO: (*aside*) He is some scoundrel. (*aloud*) Hey! no; master mysterious one! Speak without being interfered with, if you can.

COUNT: (*aside*) Cursed old man! (*aloud*) Don Bazile commissioned me to tell you . . .

BARTHOLO: Speak aloud, I am deaf in one ear.

COUNT: (*raising his voice*) Ah! willingly. That Count Almaviva, who was lodging in the Plaza . . .

BARTHOLO: (*frightened*) Speak low, speak low.

COUNT: (*louder*) Has moved this morning. As it was through me that he learned that Count Almaviva . . .

BARTHOLO: Low, speak low, I beg you.

COUNT: (*in the same tone*) . . . Was in this town, and

that I have discovered that Miss Rosine has written to him . . .

BARTHOLO: Has written to him? My dear friend, speak lower, I beg of you. There, let us sit down and have a friendly chat. You have discovered, you say, that Rosine . . .

COUNT: (*haughtily*) Assuredly. Bazile, uneasy on your account about this correspondence, had begged me to show you the letter; but the way in which you take things . . .

BARTHOLO: Hey! my dear! I take them well. But isn't it possible for you to speak lower?

COUNT: You are deaf in one ear, you have said.

BARTHOLO: Pardon, pardon, Master Alonzo, if you have found me distrustful and harsh; but I am so surrounded by intriguers and snares . . . And then, your form, your age, your air . . . Pardon, pardon. Well, you have the letter?

COUNT: It's all right with this tone, sir; but I fear that someone may be eavesdropping.

BARTHOLO: Well! who do you think? All my servants are worn out! Rosine has locked herself up in a rage! The devil has entered my house. Still I am going to make sure . . . (*He goes to open* ROSINE'S *door softly.*)

COUNT: (*aside*) I have given myself away because of spite . . . Shall I keep the letter now! I shall have to run away. I might as well not have come . . . Show it to him . . . If I can warn Rosine, to show it is a master stroke.

BARTHOLO: (*comes back on tiptoe*) She is sitting next to

her window with her back turned toward the door, busy rereading a letter from her cousin, the officer, which I had unsealed . . . Please, let's see hers.

COUNT: (*hands him* ROSINE's *letter*) Here it is. (*aside*) It is my letter which she is reading.

BARTHOLO: (*reads*) "Since you have told me your name and rank . . ." Ah! the false-hearted one. That is, indeed, her hand.

COUNT: (*frightened*) It is your turn to speak low.

BARTHOLO: What an obligation, my dear chap!

COUNT: When everything is finished, if you believe you are indebted to me, you are free to recompense me . . . According to a work that Don Bazile is now carrying on with a lawyer . . .

BARTHOLO: With a lawyer, for my marriage?

COUNT: No doubt. He charged me to tell you that all can be ready for tomorrow. Then, if she resists . . .

BARTHOLO: She will resist.

COUNT: (*wants to regain the letter, but* BARTHOLO *clasps it*) That's the time when I can serve you, we will show her letter to her, and, if necessary (*more mysteriously*), I shall go so far as to tell her that I got it from a woman to whom the count had given it; you see that worry, shame, spite may cause her immediately . . .

BARTHOLO: (*laughing*) Slander! my dear friend, now I see that you really come from Bazile . . . But, in order that this might not look as if planned in advance, would it not be well if she knew you beforehand?

COUNT: (*represses a fit of joy*) That was certainly Don Bazile's opinion. But how shall we do it? It is late . . . In the little time that is left . . .

BARTHOLO: I shall say that you are coming in his place. Will you not give her a lesson?

COUNT: There is nothing that I would not do to please you. But take care that all these stories of would-be teachers are old dodges, comedy tricks. Suppose she suspects? . . .

BARTHOLO: Introduced by me? With your appearance; you look more like a disguised lover than an obliging friend.

COUNT: Really? Do you believe my mien may aid the deceit?

BARTHOLO: I shall defy the shrewdest one to guess it. She is in a horrible mood this evening. But if she would only see you . . . Her harpsichord is in this room. Amuse yourself while you wait; I am going to do the impossible to bring her to you.

COUNT: Take good care not to speak to her of the letter.

BARTHOLO: Before the decisive moment? It would lose all its effect. One must not tell me things twice, one must not tell me things twice. (*Exit.*)

SCENE 3

THE COUNT: (*alone*) Saved at last. Phew! How hard is this devilish man to handle! Figaro knows him well. I could see myself as I lied; I surely looked flat and awkward; and he has eyes! . . . My word, without the sudden inspiration of the letter, I must confess, I would have been led out like a fool. O Heaven! they are quarreling in there. If she were to persist in refusing to come! Let us listen . . . She refuses to come out of her room, and I have lost all the advantage of my ruse. (*He listens again.*) Here she is; let us appear at first. (*He goes into the cabinet.*)

SCENE 4

THE COUNT, ROSINE, BARTHOLO

ROSINE: (*with a feigned anger*) All you will say is useless, sir, I have made up my mind, I do not want to hear anything more about music.

BARTHOLO: Please listen, my child; it is Master Alonzo, the pupil and friend of Don Bazile, chosen by him to be one of your witnesses.—Music will calm you, I assure you.

ROSINE: Oh! as for that, you can give up the idea; if I sing this evening! . . . Where is this teacher whom you fear to send away? In a few words I shall send him about his business and Bazile's too. (*She perceives her sweetheart. She utters a cry.*)

BARTHOLO: What is the matter with you?

ROSINE: (*pressing her two hands upon her heart, greatly disturbed*) Ah! Heavens, sir . . . Ah! Heavens, sir!

BARTHOLO: She is ill again . . . , Master Alonzo?

ROSINE: No, I am not ill . . . but as I turned . . . Ah!

COUNT: You turned your ankle, madam?

ROSINE: Ah! yes, I turned my ankle. I've had a horrible pain.

COUNT: I surely noticed it.

ROSINE: (*looking at the* COUNT) It struck my heart.

BARTHOLO: A chair, a chair! And not an armchair here?

COUNT: Ah! Rosine!

ROSINE: What an imprudence!

COUNT: I have a thousand important things to tell you.

ROSINE: He will not leave us.

COUNT: Figaro is going to help us.

BARTHOLO: (*brings an armchair*) There, darling, sit down. It is quite unlikely, bachelor, that she will take a lesson this evening; it will be for some other day. Farewell.

ROSINE: (*to the* COUNT) No, wait, my pain has eased a little. (*To* BARTHOLO.) I feel that I was wrong with you, sir. I want to follow your example by making amends at once . . .

BARTHOLO: Oh! what a good little nature women have! But after such pain, my child, I shall not permit you to make the least effort. Farewell, farewell, bachelor.

ROSINE: (*to the* COUNT) A moment, sir, please! (*To* BARTHOLO) I shall believe, sir, that you do not like to oblige me if you prevent me from proving my regret by my taking a lesson.

COUNT: (*aside to* BARTHOLO) Let us not oppose her if you want my advice.

BARTHOLO: That is enough, sweetheart. I am so far from trying to displease you that I want to remain here all the time you are going to study.

ROSINE: No, sir: I know that music has no attraction for you.

BARTHOLO: I assure you that she will charm me this evening.

ROSINE: (*aside to the* COUNT) I am in torment.

COUNT: (*taking up a sheet of music from the desk*) Do you want to sing that, madam?

ROSINE: Yes, it is a very pleasant piece of *The Useless Precaution.*

BARTHOLO: Still *The Useless Precaution?*

COUNT: It is the newest thing of the day. It is a picture of spring, in quite a lively *genre.* Does madam want to try it?

ROSINE: (*looking at the* COUNT) With great pleasure; a picture of spring will delight me; it is the youth of nature. After the winter, it seems that the heart acquires a higher degree of sensitivity, as a slave who has been long confined, enjoys with more pleasure the charm of liberty which has just been offered to him.

BARTHOLO: (*in a low voice to the* COUNT) Her head is always full of romantic notions.

COUNT: (*in a low voice*) Do you see the point of it?

BARTHOLO: Why, of course! (*He goes and sits down in the armchair* ROSINE *has been occupying.*)

ROSINE: (*sings*)

When o'er the plain
Love doth bring
The spring,
By lovers so cherished;
Then everything
With new life thrills,
The flowers it fills
And maketh young hearts sing.
The flocks one sees
Issuing from the hamlets.
In all the hills
The lamb's cries
Resound;
They bound.
All things are fermenting;
All things are augmenting.
The grazing sheep,
The blooming flowers,
The faithful dogs
On them watch keep.
But Lindor, passion-moved,
Scarcely thinks
But of the joy of being loved
By his shepherdess.

SAME ARIA

Far from her mother,
This shepherdess
Goes singing
To her waiting lover.
By this device
Love doth entice;
But will singing

Save one from danger?
The sweet piping reeds,
The songs of the birds,
Her growing charms,
Her fifteen or sixteen years—
Everything excites her,
All agitates her;
The poor little thing
Suffers uneasiness.
From his retreat
Lindor doth gaze;
As she advances,
Lindor leaps to her.
He has just embraced her.
She, although pleased,
Feigns a sudden anger
In order to be teased.

REFRAIN

Now sighs,
Sweet cares, fond vows,
Lively tenderness,
Pleasures,
Dear dalliance
Are put to use.
Soon our shepherdess
Feels no more anger.
If some jealous swain
Dare trouble such sweet pain,
Our lovers agreed,
Have an extreme need. . . . .
. . . . . Their joys to conceal,
But when one is in love,

Fortune can naught but feed
The great pleasures we feel.

(*As he listens,* BARTHOLO *dozes off. The* COUNT, *during the refrain, ventures to seize one of her hands, which he covers with kisses. In her emotion,* ROSINE's *song dies down until it ceases completely in the middle of the cadence at the word,* extreme. *The orchestra follows the movement of the singer, weakens with her interpretation, and is silent with her. The absence of the noise which had put* BARTHOLO *to sleep awakens him. The* COUNT *gets up,* ROSINE *and the orchestra suddenly continue the aria. If the refrain is repeated, the same action begins again, etc.*)

COUNT: Truly, it is a charming piece, and madam sings it with understanding . . .

ROSINE: You flatter me, sir; the praises belong entirely to the composer.

BARTHOLO: (*yawning*) I believe I have slept a bit during the charming piece. I have my patients. I go and come, I spin round, and, as soon as I sit down, my poor legs . . . (*He gets up and pushes away the armchair.*)

ROSINE: (*in a low voice to the* COUNT) Figaro does not come.

COUNT: Let us kill time.

BARTHOLO: But, bachelor, I have already told it to that old Bazile: is there no way of making her study things that are gayer than all these grand arias, which go up and down, rolling along with a hi, ho, a, a, a, a, and which seem to me like so many funerals? Now, some of those little airs that they used to sing in my youth, and which everybody remembered easily. I used to know some years ago . . . For instance . . . (*During the refrain, he seeks the aria, scratching his head, and sings snapping his thumbs and dancing with knees bent in the manner of old men.*)

> Do you, my Rosinette,
> Want to purchase
> The prince of spouses? . . . . .

(*To the* count, *laughing.*) There is Fanchonette in the song, but I substituted Rosinette to make it more pleasing for her and to make it fit the circumstances. Ha! ha! ha! Yes, all for the best.

SCENE 5

FIGARO, *in the back;* ROSINE, BARTHOLO, THE COUNT
BARTHOLO: (*sings*)

> Do you, my Rosinette,
> Want to purchase
> The prince of spouses?
> I am not Thyrsis; yet when
> Night falls, in the shadow,
> I am still worth my price;
> And, when it becomes dark,
> The finest cats are gray.

(*He repeats the refrain, dancing.* FIGARO, *behind him, imitates his movements.*) I am not Thyrsis, etc.

(*Perceiving* FIGARO.) Ah! Enter, master barber; come forward, you are charming!

FIGARO: (*salutes*) Sir, it is true that my mother told me so years ago; but I am a bit deformed since that time. (*Aside to the* COUNT.) Bravo, my lord. (*During all this scene, the* COUNT *does what he can to speak to* ROSINE, *but the restless and vigilant eye of the guardian always prevents him, which forms a sort of dumb show of all the actors not taking part in the repartee between the doctor and* FIGARO.)

BARTHOLO: Have you come again to purge, bleed, drug, and lay low the whole household?

FIGARO: Sir, it is not a holiday every day; but, without counting daily attentions, you may have seen that when they are needed, my zeal does not wait for your command . . .

BARTHOLO: Your zeal does not wait? What will you say, master zealot, to that poor wretch who yawns and sleeps, though wide awake? And the other; who, for the last three hours, has been sneezing to crack his skull and blow out his brains! what will you say to them?

FIGARO: What shall I say to them?

BARTHOLO: Yes!

FIGARO: Well, I shall say . . . Of course! I shall say to the one who sneezes "God bless you," and "Go to bed" to the one who yawns. It is not that, sir, that will increase the bill.

BARTHOLO: Of course not; but it is the bleeding and the medicines which will increase it, if I would permit it. Is it through zeal, too, that you have packed my mule's eyes, and will your poultice give it back its sight?

FIGARO: If it does not restore the sight, neither will it prevent it from seeing.

BARTHOLO: Let me find it in the bill! . . . One can't be that insane!

FIGARO: Indeed yes, sir, men having hardly to choose except between stupidity and folly, in which I see no profit. I want at least some pleasures; and long live joy! Who knows if the world will last three weeks longer!

BARTHOLO: You would do much better, master reasoner, to pay me my hundred crowns and the interest without trifling, I warn you.

FIGARO: Do you doubt my probity, sir? Your hundred crowns! I would rather owe them to you all my life than deny them for a single instant.

BARTHOLO: And do tell me how Miss Figaro liked the bonbons that you took her?

FIGARO: What bonbons? What do you mean?

BARTHOLO: Yes, those bonbons, in that bag made from a sheet of letter paper, this morning.

FIGARO: The devil take me if . . .

ROSINE: (*interrupting him*) Did you take care at least to tell her that they were from me, Master Figaro! I had begged you to do so.

FIGARO: Ah, ah! This morning's bonbons? How stupid I am! I had quite forgotten about them . . . Oh! excellent, madam, admirable.

BARTHOLO: Excellent! Admirable! Yes, no doubt, barber, retrace your steps! That is a fine business, sir!

FIGARO: Well, what is the matter, sir?

BARTHOLO: And which will give you a fine reputation, sir!

FIGARO: I shall try to live up to it, sir!

BARTHOLO: Say that you will live it down, sir!

FIGARO: As you please, sir!

BARTHOLO: You are putting on some airs, sir! Know that when I dispute with an ass, I never yield to him.

FIGARO: (*turns his back upon him*) We differ in that, sir! I always yield to him.

BARTHOLO: Hey, what does he mean by that, bachelor?

FIGARO: It's that you believe you have to deal with some village barber, who knows only how to handle the razor. Learn, sir, that I worked with my pen in Madrid, and that were it not for the envious . . .

BARTHOLO: Hey! why did you not remain there, without coming here to change your profession?

FIGARO: One does what one can; put yourself in my place.

BARTHOLO: Put myself in your place! Ah! to be sure, I would say a fine lot of nonsense!

FIGARO: Sir, you do not begin too badly; I leave it to your colleague, who is dreaming there.

COUNT: (*coming back to him*) I . . . I am not his colleague.

FIGARO: No? Seeing you here in consultation, I thought you were pursuing the same object.

BARTHOLO: (*angry*) Well, what brings you here? Is it to bring madam some other letter this evening? Speak, must I go?

FIGARO: How harshly you treat the poor world! Hey! to be sure, sir, I come to shave you, that's all. Isn't today your day?

BARTHOLO: You will come back later.

FIGARO: Ah! yes, come back! The whole garrison takes medicine tomorrow morning; I got the contract through my connections. Consider, then, how much time I have to lose! Are you going into your room, sir?

BARTHOLO: No, I am not going into my room. But why . . . who prevents *my* being shaved here?

ROSINE: (*scornfully*) You are polite! And why not in my apartment?

BARTHOLO: You are getting angry? Pardon, my child, you are going to finish taking your lesson! it is in order not to lose for a moment the pleasure of hearing you.

FIGARO: (*whispers to the* COUNT) You cannot get him out of here! (*aloud*) Come, L'Éveillé, La Jeunesse; the basin, the water, everything that the master needs.

BARTHOLO: That's all right, call them! Fatigued, harassed, black and blue at your hands, did they not need to go to bed?

FIGARO: Well! I shall go and look for everything; is it not

in your room? (*In a low voice to the* COUNT.) I am going to lure him out.

BARTHOLO: (*unfastens his bunch of keys and reflecting*) No, no, I'll go there myself. (*He whispers to the* COUNT *as he goes away.*) Have your eyes on them, I beg of you.

SCENE 6

FIGARO, THE COUNT, ROSINE

FIGARO: Ah! what a brilliant opportunity we have missed! He was going to give me the bunch of keys. Was not the key of the blinds among them?

ROSINE: It is the newest of all.

SCENE 7

BARTHOLO, FIGARO, THE COUNT, ROSINE

BARTHOLO: (*coming back; aside*) Good! I don't know what I am doing in having that cursed barber here. (*To* FIGARO.) Here. (*He gives him the bunch of keys.*) In my room, under my bureau; but touch nothing else.

FIGARO: A plague take you! It would be good for you, distrustful that you are! (*Aside as he goes off.*) See how Heaven protects innocence!

SCENE 8

BARTHOLO, THE COUNT, ROSINE

BARTHOLO: (*whispers to the* COUNT) He is the black-guard who took the letter to the count.

COUNT: (*in a low voice*) He looks like a scoundrel to me.

BARTHOLO: He will not catch me any more.

COUNT: I believe that as far as that is concerned, the worst is over.

BARTHOLO: All considered, I thought it more prudent to send him to my room than leave him with her.

COUNT: They would not have said a word without my having been a party to it.

ROSINE: It is quite polite, gentlemen, to speak low continually! And my lesson? (*Here one hears a noise as of dishes upset.*)

BARTHOLO: (*with a cry*) What do I hear! The cruel barber must have dropped everything downstairs and the finest pieces in my dressing-case! (*He runs outside.*)

SCENE 9

THE COUNT, ROSINE

COUNT: Let us take advantage of the moments which Figaro's intelligence has procured us. Grant me this evening, I beg you, madam, one moment's conversation, which is quite necessary to shield you from the slavery to which you are destined.

ROSINE: Ah, Lindor!

COUNT: I can climb to your blinds; and as to the letter I received from you this morning, I found myself forced . . .

SCENE 10

ROSINE, BARTHOLO, FIGARO, THE COUNT

BARTHOLO: I had not been mistaken; everything is broken, smashed.

FIGARO: It must be a great catastrophe for so much bother! You don't see at all on the stairs. (*He shows the key to the* COUNT.) As I climbed up the stairs, I caught a key . . .

BARTHOLO: You must take care of what you are doing. Catch a key! The clever man!

FIGARO: Indeed, sir, look for a more subtle one.

SCENE 11

THE PRECEDING ACTORS, DON BAZILE

ROSINE: (*aside in fright*) Don Bazile! . . .
COUNT: (*aside*) Merciful Heaven!

FIGARO: (*aside*) It is the devil!

BARTHOLO: (*goes to meet him*) Ah! Bazile, my friend, you feel quite recovered. So your accident has had no bad consequences? Truly, Master Alonzo had frightened me very much about your condition, ask him, I was leaving to come see you; and if he had not held me back . . .

BAZILE: (*astounded*) Master Alonzo? . . .

FIGARO (*stamps his foot*) Hey what! still more hitches? Two hours for one bad beard . . . Confound such a clientele!

BAZILE: (*looking at everybody*) Will you be so good as to tell me, sirs . . . ?

FIGARO: You may speak to him when I am gone.

BAZILE: But still it would be necessary . . .

COUNT: You should keep quiet, Bazile. Do you believe you are teaching him something that he does not know? I told him that you had requested me to come and give a music lesson in your place.

BAZILE: (*more astonished*) The music lesson! . . . Alonzo! . . .

ROSINE: (*aside to* BAZILE) Come! Be still.

BAZILE: She, too!

COUNT: (*in a low voice to* BARTHOLO) Please whisper to him that we have agreed.

BARTHOLO: (*aside to* BAZILE) Don't contradict us; Bazile, by saying that he is not your pupil; you would spoil everything.

BAZILE: Ha! ha!

BARTHOLO: (*aloud*) Really, Bazile, no one has more talent than your pupil.

BAZILE: (*aghast*) Than my pupil! . . . (*In a low voice.*) I came to tell you that the count has moved.

BARTHOLO: (*in a low voice*) Silence, I know it.

BAZILE: (*in a low voice*) Who told you?

BARTHOLO: (*in a low voice*) He, evidently!

COUNT: (*in a low voice*) I, no doubt: if you would only listen.

ROSINE: (*in a low voice to* BAZILE) Is it so hard for you to keep quiet?

FIGARO: (*in a low voice to* BAZILE) Hm! what a great lout! He is deaf.

BAZILE: (*aside*) Who the deuce are they deceiving here? Everybody is in the secret!

BARTHOLO: (*aloud*) Well, Bazile, your lawyer . . . ?

FIGARO: You have all evening to talk of the lawyer.

BARTHOLO: (*to* BAZILE) One word only; tell me simply whether you are satisfied with the lawyer?

BAZILE: (*terrified*) With the lawyer?

COUNT: (*smiling*) You did not see the lawyer?

BAZILE: (*impatient*) No, I did not see the lawyer.

COUNT: (*aside to* BARTHOLO) Do you want him to explain himself before her? Send him away.

BARTHOLO: (*in a whisper to the* COUNT) You are right. (*To* BAZILE.) But what sickness has come over you so suddenly?

BAZILE: (*angry*) I don't understand you.

COUNT: (*aside, puts a purse into his hand*) Yes, he has just asked you what you have come to do here, in your state of sickness.

FIGARO: He is as pale as a dead man!

BAZILE: Ah! I understand . . .

COUNT: Go to bed, my dear Bazile: you are not well and you give us an awful fright. Go to bed.

ROSINE: Why did you come out? They say that it is catching. Go to bed.

BAZILE: (*more amazed than ever*) I, go to bed?

ALL THE ACTORS TOGETHER: Oh, no doubt.

BAZILE: (*looking at them all*) In fact, lady and gentlemen, I believe I shall not do badly to retire; I feel as if I were a bit out of sorts.

BARTHOLO: Till tomorrow, as always, if you are better.

COUNT: Bazile! I shall be at your house very early tomorrow.

FIGARO: Believe me, keep yourself quite warm in your bed.

ROSINE: Good evening, Master Bazile.

BAZILE: (*aside*) The devil take me if I understand anything about it, and if it were not for the purse . . .

ALL: Good evening, Bazile, good evening.

BAZILE: (*going away*) Well! good evening, then, good evening. (*They all accompany him laughing.*)

SCENE 12

THE PRECEDING ACTORS, *except* BAZILE

BARTHOLO: (*with importance*) That man is not at all well.

ROSINE: His eyes are wild.

COUNT: He must have caught a chill.

FIGARO: Did you see how he spoke to himself? Poor mortals that we are! (*To* BARTHOLO.) Now, are you going to make up your mind this time? (*He pushes over an armchair to her a great distance from the* COUNT *and hands him the linen.*)

COUNT: Before we finish, madam, I must tell you one thing which is essential for progress in the art that I have the honor to teach you. (*He approaches her and whispers in her ear.*)

BARTHOLO: (*to* FIGARO) Come now! It seems as if you were doing it on purpose to approach me and to stand before me to prevent me from seeing . . .

COUNT: (*in a low voice to* ROSINE) We have the key to the blinds, and we shall be here at midnight.

FIGARO: (*puts the linen around* BARTHOLO's *neck*) See what? If it were a dancing lesson, we might let you look at it; but singing! . . . Goodness gracious!

BARTHOLO: What is it?

FIGARO: I don't know what has gotten into my eye. (*He brings his head nearer.*)

BARTHOLO: Don't rub so hard.

FIGARO: It's the left eye. Would you be so kind as to blow a little harder? (BARTHOLO *takes* FIGARO's *head, looks over it, pushes him away violently, and steals behind the lovers to listen to their conversation.*)

COUNT: (*in a low voice to* ROSINE) And as for your letter, I found myself a little while ago in such confusion for an excuse to remain here . . .

FIGARO: (*from a distance to warn them*) Ahem! . . . Ahem!

COUNT: Grieved also at seeing my disguise useless.

BARTHOLO: (*slipping between them*) Your disguise useless!

ROSINE: (*frightened*) Oh! . . .

BARTHOLO: Very well, madam, do not trouble yourself. What! under my very eyes, in my presence, one dares to insult me in that manner!

COUNT: What is the matter with you, sir?

BARTHOLO: Perfidious Alonzo!

COUNT: Master Bartholo, if you often have caprices like the one of which chance makes me a witness, I no longer wonder at the aversion that the young lady has to becoming your wife.

ROSINE: His wife! I! Spend my days in the company of a jealous old man, who, for its only happiness, offers my youth an abominable slavery!

BARTHOLO: Ah! what do I hear!

ROSINE: Yes, I say so aloud: I will give my heart and my hand to the one who can free me from this terrible individual, where my person and my property are detained in defiance of all laws.   (*Exit* ROSINE.)

SCENE 13

BARTHOLO, FIGARO, THE COUNT

BARTHOLO: I am choking with anger.

COUNT: Indeed, sir, it is difficult for a young woman . . .

FIGARO: Yes, a young woman and old age, that is what confuses the minds of old men.

BARTHOLO: What! when I catch them redhanded! cursed barber! I feel like . . .

FIGARO: I am going, he is insane.

COUNT: And I also; upon my word, he is insane.

FIGARO: He is insane, he is insane . . . (*Exeunt.*)

SCENE 14

BARTHOLO: (*alone, pursues them*) I am insane! Infamous instigators! Emissaries of the devil, whose errands you are doing here and may he take you all! . . . I am insane! . . . I saw them as clearly as I see this desk . . .

and to uphold brazenly! . . . Ah! Bazile is the only one who can explain this to me. Yes, let's send for him. Ho there, somebody! . . . Ah! I forgot that I have nobody . . . A neighbor, the first who comes along, I don't care who. It's enough to make me lose my mind! It's enough to make me lose my mind!

During the intermission the stage grows dark; the noise of a storm is heard, and the orchestra plays what is noted in the collection of music for The Barber.

ACT FOUR

The stage is dark.

SCENE I

BARTHOLO, DON BAZILE, *a paper lantern in his hand*

BARTHOLO: What, Bazile, you do not know him? Is what you tell me possible?

BAZILE: If you should ask me a hundred times, I should always give you the same answer. If he handed Rosine's letter over to you, he is no doubt one of the count's emissaries. But, to judge from the magnificence of the present he made, it could very well be the count himself.

BARTHOLO: Apropos of that present, hey! why did you take it?

BAZILE: You looked as if you were in agreement; I did not understand anything about it; and in cases hard to decide, a purse of gold always appears to me an unanswerable argument. And then, as the proverb says, what is good to take . . .

BARTHOLO: I understand, is good . . .

BAZILE: To keep.

BARTHOLO: (*surprised*) Ha! ha!

BAZILE: Yes, I have arranged several little proverbs like

that with variations. But let us come to the point: what have you decided?

BARTHOLO: If you were in my place, Bazile, would you not make extreme efforts to keep her in your power?

BAZILE: Indeed no, doctor. In all kinds of property, possession amounts to little; it is their enjoyment which makes one happy: my opinion is that marrying a woman who does not love you is only to expose yourself . . .

BARTHOLO: You would fear mishaps?

BAZILE: Well! well! sir . . . one sees many of them in this year. I would not do violence to her heart.

BARTHOLO: Your servant, Bazile. It is better for her to cry possessing me, than for me to die of grief at not having her.

BAZILE: So it is a matter of life and death? Marry, doctor, marry.

BARTHOLO: I shall do so, and this very night.

BAZILE: Farewell, then.—Remember, when speaking to your ward, to paint them all blacker than hell.

BARTHOLO: You are right.

BAZILE: Slander, doctor, slander. One must always come to that.

BARTHOLO: Here is Rosine's letter which that Alonzo handed over to me, and he showed me, without wishing to, the use I must make of it with her.

BAZILE: Farewell; we shall all be here at four o'clock.[1]

BARTHOLO: Why not earlier?

---

[1] *Four o'clock is in reality past midnight. It is* quatre heures *after dark.*

BAZILE: Impossible; the notary[2] is engaged.

BARTHOLO: For a marriage?

BAZILE: Yes, at the barber Figaro's; he is marrying off his niece.

BARTHOLO: His niece? He hasn't any.

BAZILE: That is what they said to the notary.

BARTHOLO: That knave is the plot, what the devil!

BAZILE: Would you think . . . ?

BARTHOLO: Indeed, those fellows are so alert! Look here, my friend, I am uneasy. Return to the notary's. Come back with him at once.

BAZILE: It rains, the weather is infernal; but nothing will stop me in your service. What are you doing?

BARTHOLO: I'll show you out. Haven't they made Figaro cripple all my servants! I am alone here.

BAZILE: I have my lantern.

BARTHOLO: There, Bazile, there is my passkey. I shall wait for you, I shall watch; and come who will, except the notary and you, no one will get in tonight.

BAZILE: With these precautions, you are sure of yourself.

SCENE 2

ROSINE: (*alone, coming out of her room*) It seems to me I heard talking. It has just struck midnight; Lindor is not

---

[2] *In France a* notaire *must have a law degree. One of his functions is signing marriage contracts, in which the dowry plays a large part.*

coming! This bad weather was the very thing to help him. Sure of meeting nobody . . . Ah! Lindor! if you had deceived me! What noise do I hear? . . . Goodness gracious! it is my guardian. Let us go back.

SCENE 3

ROSINE, BARTHOLO

BARTHOLO: (*comes back with some light*) Ah! Rosine, since you have not yet retired to your apartment . . .

ROSINE: I am going to retire.

BARTHOLO: In this horrible weather you will not get any rest, and I have very urgent things to tell you.

ROSINE: What do you want from me, sir? Is it not enough to be tormented by day?

BARTHOLO: Rosine, listen to me.

ROSINE: Tomorrow I'll listen to you.

BARTHOLO: One moment, please.

ROSINE: (*aside*) Suppose he were to come!

BARTHOLO: (*shows her her letter*) Do you recognize this letter?

ROSINE: (*recognizes it*) Ah! Great Heaven!

BARTHOLO: My intention, Rosine, is not to reproach you: at your age one may be led astray; but I am your friend, listen to me.

ROSINE: I can't bear it any longer.

BARTHOLO: That letter which you wrote to Count Almaviva . . .

ROSINE: (*astonished*) To Count Almaviva!

BARTHOLO: Now see what a horrible fellow this Count is: as soon as he received it he made a trophy of it; I have it from a woman to whom he gave it.

ROSINE: Count Almaviva! . . .

BARTHOLO: You have difficulty in convincing yourself that it is so horrible. Inexperience, Rosine, makes your sex trusting and credulous; but learn into what a snare they were drawing you. That woman has warned me of everything, apparently to cast aside a rival so dangerous as you. I shudder at the thought! The most abominable plot among Almaviva, Figaro, and that Alonzo, that would-be pupil of Bazile's, who bears another name and is only the base agent of the Count, was going to drag you in an abyss from which nothing could have drawn you out.

ROSINE: (*overwhelmed*) How horrible! . . . What! Lindor? . . . what! that young man . . . ?

BARTHOLO: (*aside*) Ah! it is Lindor.

ROSINE: It is for Count Almaviva . . . it is for another . . .

BARTHOLO: That is what they told me when they gave me your letter.

ROSINE: (*in an outrage*) Ah! what a vileness! . . . He shall be punished for it.—Sir, you have expressed the desire to marry me?

BARTHOLO: You know the depth of my feelings.

ROSINE: If there are any feelings left, I am yours.

BARTHOLO: Well! the notary will come this very evening.

ROSINE: That is not all. O Heaven! am I not humiliated enough! . . . Know that in a little while the villain will dare enter by these blinds, whose key they have artfully stolen from you.

BARTHOLO: (*looking at his bunch of keys*) Ah! the villains! My child, I will leave you no more.

ROSINE: (*in fright*) Ah! sir, and suppose they are armed?

BARTHOLO: You are right: I would lose my revenge. Go up to Marceline: lock yourself up in her room with a double lock. I am going to call the police, and wait for him near the house. He will be arrested like a thief, and we shall have the pleasure of being at once avenged and delivered from him! And remember that my love will make amends to you . . .

ROSINE: (*in despair*) Forget only my error. (*aside*) Ah! I am punished enough for it!

BARTHOLO: (*going away*) Let us go and lie in wait. At last I have her. (*Exit.*)

SCENE 4

ROSINE: (*alone*) His love will make amends to me . . . Wretch that I am! . . . (*She draws her handkerchief and gives way to tears.*) What shall I do? . . . He will be coming. I want to remain and pretend with him in order to contemplate him for a moment in all his blackness. The vileness of his actions will be my preserver . . . Ah! I greatly need one. What a noble face! a gentle air! a voice so tender! . . . and he is only the mean agent of a corrupter. Ah! unfortunate one that I am! . . . Heaven! someone is opening the blinds. (*She escapes.*)

SCENE 5

THE COUNT, FIGARO, *wrapped in a mantle, appears at the window*

FIGARO: (*speaks outside*) Someone is fleeing; shall I enter?

COUNT: (*outside*) A man?

FIGARO: No.

COUNT: It is Rosine, whom your hideous face must have put to flight.

FIGARO: (*leaps into the room*) Indeed, I believe so . . . Here we are at last, in spite of the rain, the thunder, and the lightning.

COUNT: (*wrapped in a long mantle*) Give me your hand. (*He also leaps.*) Victory!

FIGARO: (*throws off the mantle*) We are quite drenched. Charming weather to go on love errands! My lord, how do you like the night?

COUNT: Splendid for a lover.

FIGARO: Yes, but for a confidant? . . . And suppose someone were to surprise us here?

COUNT: Are you not with me? I have quite a different anxiety: that is, to prevail upon her to leave her guardian's home at once.

FIGARO: You have working for you three passions all-powerful over the fair sex: love, hate, and fear.

COUNT: (*looks into the darkness*) How shall I tell her brusquely that the notary is waiting for her at your house to unite us? She will find my plan quite bold. She is going to call me audacious.

FIGARO: If she calls you audacious, you will call her cruel. Women like very much to be called cruel. Moreover, if your love is as strong as you desire it to be, you will tell her who you are: she will no longer doubt your feelings.

SCENE 6

THE COUNT, ROSINE, FIGARO

FIGARO *lights all the candles on the table.*

COUNT: Here she is.—My fair Rosine!

ROSINE: (*in a very impassive manner*) I began, sir, to fear that you were not coming.

COUNT: Charming anxiety! . . . Miss, it isn't suitable to take advantage of circumstances to ask you to share the lot of an unfortunate man; but, whatever asylum you may choose, I swear upon my honor . . .

ROSINE: Sir, if the gift of my hand had not had to follow at once that of my heart, you would not be here. May necessity justify in your eyes whatever irregularity there is in this interview!

COUNT: You, Rosine! the companion of an unfortunate fellow without money, without birth! . . .

ROSINE: Birth, money! Let us put aside such freaks of chance, and if you will assure me that your intentions are pure . . .

COUNT: (*at her feet*) Ah! Rosine! I adore you! . . .

ROSINE: (*indignant*) Stop, you wretch! . . . You dare to profane! . . . You adore me! . . . Go! you are no longer dangerous for me; I was waiting for this word to detest you. But, before I abandon you to the remorse which awaits you (*weeping*), learn that I did love you; learn that it would have made me happy to share your poor lot. Unfortunate Lindor! I was going to leave everything to follow you. But the cowardly abuse that you have made of my kindness and the vileness of that horrible Count Almaviva, to whom you were selling me, have brought me this testimony of my weakness. Do you recognize this letter?

COUNT: (*with animation*) Which your guardian handed to you?

ROSINE: (*proudly*) Yes, I am indebted to him for it.

COUNT: Heaven! how happy I am! He had it from me. In my embarrassment, yesterday, I made use of it to get his confidence, and I could not find the moment to tell you of it. Ah! Rosine! it is true, then, that you love me truly! . . .

FIGARO: My lord, you were seeking a woman who would love you for yourself . . .

ROSINE: My lord! what is he saying?

COUNT: (*throwing off his wide mantle, appears magnificently clothed*) O most beloved of women! it is no longer time to deceive you: the happy man you see at your feet is not Lindor; I am Count Almaviva, who loves you madly and who has been seeking you in vain for the last six months.

ROSINE: (*falls into the* COUNT's *arms*) Ah!

COUNT: (*frightened*) Figaro?

FIGARO: No uneasiness, my lord; the sweet emotion of joy never has annoying consequences. There, there, she is regaining her senses; my word! how beautiful she is!

ROSINE: Ah! Lindor! . . . Ah! sir! how guilty I am! I was going to yield to my guardian this very night.

COUNT: You, Rosine!

ROSINE: See only how I am punished! I would have spent my life in detesting you. Ah! Lindor! is it not the most terrible torture to hate, when one feels impelled to love?

FIGARO: (*looks out the window*) My lord, our return is cut off; the ladder is taken away.

COUNT: Taken away!

ROSINE: (*disturbed*) Yes, it is I . . . it is the doctor. That is the fruit of my cruelty. He deceived me. I confessed everything: he knows that you are here, and is going to come with the police.

FIGARO: (*looks out again*) My lord! someone is opening the street door.

ROSINE: (*running to the* COUNT'*s arms in fright*) Ah! Lindor!

COUNT: (*firmly*) Rosine, you love me! I do not fear anyone; and you shall be my wife. So I shall have the pleasure of punishing the odious old man as I please! . . .

ROSINE: No, no, have mercy on him, dear Lindor! My heart is so full that vengeance can find no place there.

SCENE 7

THE NOTARY, DON BAZILE, THE PRECEDING ACTORS

FIGARO: My lord, it is our notary.

COUNT: And friend Bazile with him.

BAZILE: Ah! what do I perceive?

FIGARO: Well! by what chance, our friend? . . .

BAZILE: By what chance, sir? . . .

NOTARY: Are these the future bride and groom?

COUNT: Yes, sir. You were to unite Miss Rosine and me tonight at the house of the barber Figaro; but we preferred this house for reasons which you will know later. Do you have our contract?

NOTARY: I have the honor, then, to speak to His Excellency Count Almaviva.

FIGARO: Precisely.

BAZILE: (*aside*) If it is for that reason that he gave me the passkey . . .

NOTARY: I have two marriage contracts here, my lord;

let us not confuse them: here is yours, and here is Bartholo's with Miss . . . Rosine, too. These young ladies are apparently, two sisters that bear the same name.

COUNT: Let us sign at all events. Don Bazile will be willing to serve as second witness. (*They sign.*)

BAZILE: But, Your Excellency . . . I do not understand . . .

COUNT: Master Bazile, a trifle embarrasses you, and everything astonishes you.

BAZILE: My lord . . . but suppose the doctor . . .

COUNT: (*throwing him a purse*) You are acting like a child! Sign quickly.

BAZILE: (*amazed*) Ha! ha!

FIGARO: Where is the difficulty of signing?

BAZILE: (*weighing the purse*) There is no more difficulty; but it is because once I have given my word, I need reasons of great weight . . . (*He signs.*)

SCENE 8 AND LAST

BARTHOLO, A SHERIFF, POLICEMEN, SERVANTS
with torches, and THE PRECEDING ACTORS

BARTHOLO: (*sees the* COUNT *kiss* ROSINE's *hand, and* FIGARO *grotesquely embracing* DON BAZILE: *he cries out taking the* NOTARY *by the throat*) Rosine with these scoundrels! Arrest everybody! I hold one of them by the collar.

NOTARY: It is your notary.

BAZILE: It is your notary. You're joking?

BARTHOLO: Ah! Don Bazile. How is it that you are here?

BAZILE: Rather, you, how is it that you were not here?

SHERIFF: (*pointing out* FIGARO) One moment; I know this man. What are you doing in this house at such an unearthly hour?

FIGARO: An unearthly hour! You see very well that it is as near morning as evening. Moreover, I am a retainer of His Excellency, My Lord Count Almaviva.

BARTHOLO: Almaviva!

SHERIFF: So they are not robbers?

BARTHOLO: Let us drop that.—Everywhere else, Count Almaviva, I am Your Excellency's servant; but you understand that the superiority of rank is useless here. If you please, be so good as to retire.

COUNT: Yes, rank must be useless here; but what is very powerful is the preference to you that Miss Rosine has just shown me by voluntarily giving herself to me.

BARTHOLO: What is he saying, Rosine?

ROSINE: He is telling the truth. How is it you are astonished? Was I not this very night to be avenged of a deceiver? I am.

BAZILE: When I told you that it was the Count himself, doctor.

BARTHOLO: What do I care? An absurd marriage, indeed! Where are the witnesses?

COUNT: There is nothing missing. I have been assisted by these two gentlemen.

BARTHOLO: What, Bazile! you signed?

BAZILE: What would you have? This devil of a man always has his pockets full of irresistible arguments.

BARTHOLO: I do not care about his arguments. I shall use my authority.

COUNT: You have lost it by making ill use of it.

BARTHOLO: The young lady is a minor.

FIGARO: She has just freed herself.

BARTHOLO: Who's speaking to you, you scoundrel?

COUNT: The young lady is noble and beautiful; I am a man of rank, young and rich; she is my wife; does anyone expect to dispute me this title which honors us both?

BARTHOLO: Never shall one take her from my hands.

COUNT: She is no longer in your power. I am putting her under the protection of the laws; and this gentleman, whom you have summoned yourself, will protect her from the violence to which you may want to submit her. True magistrates are the protectors of all the oppressed.

SHERIFF: Certainly. And this useless resistance to a most honorable marriage shows well enough his fright over the bad administration of his ward's property, of which he will have to render account.

COUNT: Ah! let him consent to everything, and I shall ask nothing else of him.

FIGARO: Except the receipt for my hundred crowns: let us not lose our heads.

BARTHOLO: (*angry*) They were all against me; I have thrust my head in a hornet's nest.

BAZILE: What hornet's nest! Remember, doctor, although you cannot have the woman, the money remains; and . . .

BARTHOLO: Oh! please leave me alone, Bazile! You think only of money. Little do I care for money now! Of course, I shall keep it, but do you believe that is the reason which induces me? (*He signs.*)

FIGARO: (*laughing*) Ha! ha! ha! my lord; they are of the same family.

NOTARY: But, gentlemen, I don't quite understand. Are there not two misses that bear the same name?

FIGARO: No, sir, they are only one.

BARTHOLO: (*grieving*) And it was I who took away the ladder so that the marriage should be more certain! Ah! I have ruined myself for lack of precautions.

FIGARO: For lack of good sense. But to tell the truth, doctor, when youth and love agree to deceive an old man, all he does to prevent it may justly be called *The Useless Precaution.*

THE MARRIAGE OF FIGARO

or

THE MAD DAY

CHARACTERS

COUNT ALMAVIVA, Governor of Andalusia.

THE COUNTESS, his wife.

FIGARO, the Count's valet and steward of the castle.

SUZANNE, the Countess's principal chambermaid and Figaro's fiancée.

MARCELINE, housekeeper.

ANTONIO, gardener of the castle, Suzanne's uncle, and Fanchette's father.

FANCHETTE, Antonio's daughter.

CHÉRUBIN, principal page to the Count.

BARTHOLO, a physician from Seville.

BAZILE, the Countess's harpsichord teacher.

DON GUSMAN BRID'OISON, Associate Justice of the district.

DOUBLE-MAIN, clerk and secretary to Don Gusman.

A COURT USHER.

GRIPPE-SOLEIL, a young shepherd.

A YOUNG SHEPHERDESS.

PÉDRILLE, the Count's postilion.

SILENT CHARACTERS

A TROUPE OF VALETS—A TROUPE OF PEASANTS.

The scene is in the castle of Aguas-Frescas, three leagues from Seville.

CHARACTERS AND COSTUMING
OF THE PLAY

COUNT ALMAVIVA must be played with great nobility, but also with lightness and freedom. The corruption of his heart must not remove *the good form* of his manners. In keeping with the customs *of those days,* the great considered the conquest of women a trifle. This role is all the more arduous in that the character's grandeur is always sacrificed. But in the hands of a most capable actor (like M. *Molé*)[1] the role can bring out all the others and insure the success of the play.

In the first and second acts the Count wears a hunting costume in the old Spanish style with half-boots. From the third act to the end, he wears a more magnificent version of the same costume.

THE COUNTESS, moved by two opposing sentiments, must show only a restrained feeling or a very moderate anger; nothing, above all, which lowers in the spectator's eyes her lovable and virtuous character. This role, one of the most difficult in the play, has done infinite honor to the great talent of Mlle *Saint-Val* junior.

The Countess's costume in the first, second, and

---

[1] M. *Molé, Mlle Saint-Val, etc. were the first actors of* The Marriage of Figaro. *Beaumarchais must have seen them.*

fourth acts is a comfortable dressing gown. She wears no ornament on her head. She is supposed to be indisposed, and keeps to her room. In the fifth act she wears Suzanne's clothes and high hairdress.

The actor who plays FIGARO cannot be too strongly urged to become permeated with the true spirit of the character, as M. *D'Azincourt* has done. If he finds in the role nothing but reasoning spiced with gaiety and wit, if above all he allows himself the least overacting, he will demean a role which, according to the first comedian of the theatre, M. *Préville,* should honor the talent of any actor who can seize upon its manifold nuances and can sustain all the possibilities of its conception.

His clothes are the same as in *The Barber of Seville.*

SUZANNE is a clever girl, full of wit and laughter, but displaying none of the brazen gaiety of our corruptive chambermaids.

Her costume in the first four acts is a tight white bodice with flounced skirt, elegant. Her hat is a toque (later called in France *à la Suzanne*). In the festival of Act IV, the Count places on her head a toque adorned with a long veil, tall feathers, and white ribbons. In Act V she wears the Countess's dressing gown and no ornament on her head.

MARCELINE is a woman of wit, with lively instincts, but whose mistakes and experience have reformed her character. If the actress who plays this role can rise with a judicious pride to the moral height that follows the recognition scene in Act III, she will add greatly to the interest of the work.

Her costume is that of the Spanish duenna, modest in color, with a black bonnet on her head.

ANTONIO must display only a half-drunken condition, which gradually wears off, so that in Act V it is almost unnoticeable.

His clothes are those of a Spanish peasant; his sleeves hang down behind; a hat and white shoes.

FANCHETTE is a girl of twelve and very ingenuous. Her costume is a tight bodice with piping and silver buttons. Her skirt is of a garish color. She wears a black toque with feathers. The other peasant girls in the wedding party are dressed like her.

The role of CHÉRUBIN cannot be played as it has been, except by a young and very pretty woman. We have no very young man on our stage who is educated enough to feel the subtleties of the part. Excessively timid before the Countess, he is elsewhere a charming scamp; a vague restless desire is at the bottom of his character. He rushes headlong through adolescence, but without any plan, without knowledge, and entirely the plaything of each passing event. In short, he is perhaps what every mother, at bottom, would like her son to be, even though she must suffer for it a great deal.

In the first and second acts, Chérubin's rich costume

is the court dress of a Spanish page, white and trimmed with silver; a light blue cloak on the shoulders and a hat with large plumes. In Act IV, he wears the bodice, skirt, and toque of the peasant girls who bring him; in Act V, an officer's uniform, a cockade, and a sword.

The character and costume of BARTHOLO are the same as in *The Barber of Seville*. In the present play, his role is secondary.

BAZILE's character and costume are the same as in *The Barber of Seville*. In the present play, his role, too, is secondary.

DON GUSMAN BRID'OISON must have the easy and open self-assurance of animals which no longer have their shyness. His stuttering is an additional charm, hardly noticeable at all. The actor would be gravely mistaken and would misconstrue the role if he sought to stress what is ludicrous in it. The part is entirely in the contrast between the solemnity of his office and the absurdity of the character, and the less the actor will overact it, the more truly he will show his talent.

His costume is the robe of a Spanish judge, but not as full as that of our state's attorneys, almost a cassock; a large wig, a neck band or ruff Spanish style, and a long white wand.

DOUBLE-MAIN is dressed like the justice, but carries a shorter wand.

THE USHER or ALGUAZIL wears a coat, mantle, Crispin sword,[2] but carried at his side without a leather belt. No boots, black shoes, a long white curly wig, and a short white wand.

GRIPPE-SOLEIL wears peasant clothes, sleeves hanging down, a gaudy jacket, a white hat.

A YOUNG SHEPHERDESS's costume is like Fanchette's.

PÉDRILLE wears a short jacket, vest, courier's whip, boots, and hat, a net over his hair.

THE SILENT CHARACTERS include some in judge's costume, others are dressed as peasants, the rest are in livery.

Where the actors are placed.

To facilitate acting, we have paid attention to writing at the beginning of each scene the names of the characters in the order in which the spectator sees them. If they do some important movement in the scene, it is indicated by a new order of names, written in a note as soon as it happens. It is important to preserve good theatrical position; the relaxation in the tradition given by the first actors produces a total effect in acting, which finally assimilates negligent troupes to the weakest actors of society.

[2] *A Crispin sword is a sword with a leather guard. Crispin was a Christian martyr, born at Soissons, France (3rd century). He was a shoemaker by trade. Crispin is also a popular valet in French comedy.*

ACT ONE

The stage represents a half-furnished room, with a large invalid chair in the center. FIGARO *is measuring the floor with a yardstick.* SUZANNE, *before a mirror, is arranging in her hair the sprig of orange blossoms usually called "the bride's bonnet."*

SCENE I

FIGARO, SUZANNE

FIGARO: Nineteen feet by twenty-six.

SUZANNE: Look, Figaro, here is my bonnet. Do you like it better this way?

FIGARO: (*takes her hands in his*) There is no comparison, my sweet. Oh! how that pretty virginal bunch of flowers, raised on the head of a lovely girl, is sweet to a groom on the morning of his wedding! . . .

SUZANNE: (*leaves*) What are you measuring there, my lad?

FIGARO: I am seeing, dear Suzy, whether this beautiful bed that my lord is giving us will fit here.

SUZANNE: In *this* room?

FIGARO: He is letting us have it.

SUZANNE: But I don't want it.

FIGARO: Why?

SUZANNE: I don't want it.

FIGARO: But why?

SUZANNE: I dislike it.

FIGARO: You might give a reason.

SUZANNE: Suppose I don't want to give any?

FIGARO: Women! When they are sure of us?

SUZANNE: To give a reason would imply that I can be wrong. Are you with me or not?

FIGARO: You are getting into a temper against the most convenient room in the castle. Moreover, it connects both suites. At night, if my lady is indisposed, she will sing; snap! there you are in two steps. Does my lord require something, he has only to ring his bell, crack! I go to him in three strides.

SUZANNE: Very well! but when he has rung in the morning to give you a good long errand, snap! in two steps he is at my door, and crack, in three strides . . .

FIGARO: What do you mean by those words?

SUZANNE: You should listen to me calmly.

FIGARO: What is the matter, good grief!

SUZANNE: The matter is, my dear, that Count Almaviva, tired of courting the beauties of the neighborhood, wants to go back home, not to *his* wife, you understand, but to yours. *She* is the one he has his eyes on, and he hopes this apartment will do no harm. And that is what the faithful Bazile, the trusted agent of the Count's pleasures and my noble singing teacher, repeats to me each day, as he gives me my lesson.

FIGARO: Bazile! my boy! If ever a shower of green birch, applied to a back, has duly corrected the curvature of some-one's spine . . .

SUZANNE: So you believed, innocent boy! that this dowry the Count is giving me was for your fine merit?

FIGARO: I had done enough to hope it was.

SUZANNE: How stupid people of wit are!

FIGARO: So they say.

SUZANNE: But *they* won't believe it!

FIGARO: *They* are wrong.

SUZANNE: Learn that he destines the dowry to get from me, secretly, a certain privilege which used to be the ancient right of the lord of the manor[1] . . . You know how grievous it was!

FIGARO: I know it so well that if the Count had not abolished that shameful right when he himself got married, I should never have wedded you on his lands.

SUZANNE: Very well, if he abolished it, he repents of it. And he wants your fiancée to restore it to him in secret today.

FIGARO: (*rubbing his head*) My head grows soft with surprise and my sprouting forehead . . .[2]

---

[1] *The alleged right to enjoy the bride of any vassal on her wedding night has no basis in fact, even though writers widely refer to it.*

[2] *This is an allusion to a cuckold. The play includes mentions of the horns of the cuckold, expressed by references to the forehead.*

SUZANNE: Please don't rub it!

FIGARO: What's the danger?

SUZANNE: (*laughing*) If there came a little pimple, superstitious people might . . .

FIGARO: You are laughing, you hussy! Ah! if there were a way of catching this professional deceiver, of making him fall into a good trap, and of pocketing his gold!

SUZANNE: Intrigue and money; now you're in your element.

FIGARO: It isn't shame that holds me back.

SUZANNE: Fear, then?

FIGARO: It is no great feat to undertake something dangerous; the thing is to escape peril and to succeed. For, to go into somebody's house at night, to enjoy his wife, and to get a hundred whiplashes for his pains, nothing is easier; a thousand knavish fools have done it. But . . . (*A bell rings inside.*)

SUZANNE: My lady is awake. She wanted me to be the first to talk to her this morning about my wedding.

FIGARO: Is there still something going on?

SUZANNE: The shepherd's almanac says that brings good luck to abandoned wives. Farewell, my sweet Fi, Fi, Figaro. Think about our business.

FIGARO: To start my brains going, give a little kiss.

SUZANNE: To my lover, today? No, sir! What would my husband say tomorrow? (FIGARO *kisses her.*)

SUZANNE: Well! well!

FIGARO: It's that you do not know how much I love you.

SUZANNE: (*adjusting her dress*) When will you, big bore, stop talking about it to me from morning till night?

FIGARO: (*mysteriously*) Why, when I can prove it to you from night till morning. (*The bell rings again.*)

SUZANNE: (*blowing him a kiss from afar*) There's your kiss, sir; I have nothing else of yours.

FIGARO: (*runs after her*) But you didn't receive mine like this.

SCENE 2

FIGARO: (*alone*) What a charming girl! Always laughing, full of sap, gaiety, wit, love, and joy! but how well-behaved! . . . (*He walks about fast, rubbing his hands.*) Ah, my lord, my dear lord! You want to give me . . . something to remember you by? I was wondering, too, why, having appointed me steward, he makes me part of the embassy and then King's Messenger. Now I understand, Your Excellency! Three promotions at once: you as envoy; I as political trouble shooter; and Suzy as lady in residence, as private ambassadress, and then, messenger, be off! While I gallop in one direction, you would make my girl ride a long way in the other! While I wade through mud, while I break my neck for the glory of your family, you will condescend to co-operate in the increase of mine! What a nice reciprocity! But, my lord, there is excess in this. To carry on in London the business of both your master and your humble servant!

to represent in a foreign court the King and me at the same time, that is too much by half, that is too much. As for you, Bazile! my fine scoundrel! I want to teach you to limp before the lame; I want . . . No, let us play along with them in order to knock both their heads together. Figaro, concentrate on this day! First, move ahead the time of your wedding, in order to make sure of it; then get rid of Marceline, who is too fond of you, pocket whatever gold and presents there may be; give the slip to the little passions of the Count; thrash Mr. Bazile soundly, and . . .

SCENE 3

MARCELINE, BARTHOLO, FIGARO

FIGARO: (*interrupts himself*) Well, well! here is the fat doctor, the party will be complete. Good morning, dear doctor of my heart. Is it my wedding with Suzy that brings you to the castle?

BARTHOLO: (*with disdain*) Not at all, my dear sir.

FIGARO: That would indeed be generous!

BARTHOLO: Of course, and therefore too stupid.

FIGARO: I had the bad luck to upset your plans! [3]

BARTHOLO: Have you anything else to say?

[3] *This is an allusion to* The Barber of Seville, *in which Figaro thwarts the plans of Bartholo, who wanted to marry his ward Rosine himself, instead of Count Almaviva. Rosine marries the latter and becomes Countess Almaviva.*

FIGARO: Your mule hasn't been cared for! [4]

BARTHOLO: (*angry*) Confounded chatterer! leave us alone.

FIGARO: You're getting angry, doctor? People of your profession are very harsh! no more pity for poor animals . . . truly . . . as if they were men! Farewell, Marceline. Do you still feel like suing me? "Although you love not, must we hate each other?" I leave it to the doctor.

BARTHOLO: What is it?

FIGARO: She will tell you anyway. (*Exit.*)

SCENE 4

MARCELINE, BARTHOLO

BARTHOLO: (*watches him go*) That fellow is always the same! And, unless someone flays him alive, I foretell that he will die in the skin of the most insolent ass I know . . .

MARCELINE: (*draws his attention*) Well, here you are at last, eternal doctor! you always so solemn and stiff that one could die waiting for your help, just as some time ago someone got married despite your precautions.[5]

BARTHOLO: Always so bitter and provoking! Well, who

---

[4] *The blind mule who is given a poultice by Figaro is referred to in* The Barber of Seville.

[5] *Rosine married Count Almaviva despite Bartholo's precautions. This is the subject of* The Barber of Seville.

makes my presence in the castle so necessary? Has the Count met with an accident?

MARCELINE: No, doctor.

BARTHOLO: And Rosine, his misleading countess, can she be, God be praised, indisposed?

MARCELINE: She is pining away.

BARTHOLO: What about?

MARCELINE: Her husband neglects her.

BARTHOLO: (*with satisfaction*) Ah! worthy husband, my avenger!

MARCELINE: One cannot make out the Count: he is a jealous man and a philanderer.

BARTHOLO: A philanderer from boredom, jealous from vanity; that goes without saying.

MARCELINE: Today, for example, he is marrying off our Suzanne to her Figaro, on whom he lavishes presents in honor of this union . . .

BARTHOLO: Which His Excellency has made necessary!

MARCELINE: Not entirely; but which event His Excellency would like to celebrate in secret with the bride . . .

BARTHOLO: Of Mr. Figaro? That's a deal you cannot conclude with him.

MARCELINE: Bazile is sure it is not so.

BARTHOLO: That other rascal lives here, too. It is a den! Well! what does he do?

MARCELINE: All the evil of which he is capable. But the worst I find is that annoying passion that he has so long nursed for me.

BARTHOLO: I should have gotten rid of his intentions many times.

MARCELINE: How?

BARTHOLO: By marrying him.

MARCELINE: Insipid and cruel wit, why don't you get rid of mine in the same way? You're in honor bound to do so. Where is the memory of your pledges? What has become of that of our little Emmanuel, the offspring of a forgotten love, which was to lead us to the altar?

BARTHOLO: (*taking off his hat*) Was it to listen to this idle talk that you had me come from Seville? And what is this fit of marrying that you have so suddenly fallen into? . . .

MARCELINE: Very well! let's not talk any further about it. But if nothing could have made you do the right thing, at least help me to marry someone else.

BARTHOLO: Ah! willingly; let's talk. But what mortal, bereft of Heaven and women, would. . . ?

MARCELINE: Now, who could it be, doctor, if not the handsome, gay, lovable Figaro?

BARTHOLO: That blackguard?

MARCELINE: Never angry, always in good humor, always ready to enjoy the passing moment, and worrying as little about the future as about the past; sprightly, generous! oh generous! . . .

BARTHOLO: Like a thief.

MARCELINE: Like a lord. Charming, in short; but he is also the greatest monster!

BARTHOLO: What about his Suzanne?

MARCELINE: She won't get him, the clever one, if you would help me, my dear doctor, and hold him to a pledge of his that I have.

BARTHOLO: On his wedding day?

MARCELINE: Marriages have gone further than this and have been broken off. If I didn't fear giving away a feminine secret! . . .

BARTHOLO: Are there any secrets from a physician?

MARCELINE: Ah! You know I have no secrets from you! my sex is ardent but shy. It is useless for a certain charm to draw us toward pleasure, the most adventurous woman hears a voice within that tells her: "Be beautiful if you can, sensible if you will, but be respected, you must." Now since every woman knows the importance of being at least respected, let us first scare off Suzanne by exposing the offers that are being made to her.

BARTHOLO: Where will that lead?

MARCELINE: That, being seized by shame, she will keep on refusing the Count, who, to avenge himself, will support my opposition to her marriage; hence mine will become a certainty.

BARTHOLO: She's right. By God! it is a good trick to marry off my old housekeeper to the rascal who took away my young ward.

MARCELINE: (quickly) And the man who means to serve his pleasures by deluding my hopes.

BARTHOLO: (*quickly*) And the man who, once upon a time, stole a hundred crowns that I haven't forgotten.

MARCELINE: Ah! what delight!

BARTHOLO: To punish a blackguard . . .

MARCELINE: To marry him, doctor, to marry him!

SCENE 5

MARCELINE, BARTHOLO, SUZANNE

SUZANNE: (*holding a bonnet with a broad ribbon and a woman's dress over her arm*) To marry him! to marry him! whom? my Figaro?

MARCELINE: (*tartly*) Why not? Aren't you planning to marry him?

BARTHOLO: (*laughing*) An angry woman's typical argument! We were speaking, my dear Suzy, of his happiness in possessing you.

MARCELINE: To say nothing of my lord.

SUZANNE: (*with a curtsy*) Your humble servant, madam;[6] there is always something bitter in your remarks.

MARCELINE: (*with a curtsy*) Your humble servant too, madam; where is the bitterness? Isn't it right for a liberal nobleman to share a little the joy he procures for his people?

---

[6] Madame, "madam," is used in French classical tragedy and comedy to address unmarried ladies as well as married ones. This is the case with Corneille, Racine, Molière, and Voltaire.

SUZANNE: He procures?

MARCELINE: Yes, madam.

SUZANNE: Luckily, your jealousy is as well known as your claims on Figaro are slight.

MARCELINE: They could have been strengthened if I had used your tactics.

SUZANNE: Ah? those tactics, madam, are those of learned ladies.

MARCELINE: But not the child! He is innocent like an old judge!

BARTHOLO: (*pulling* MARCELINE *away*) Farewell, pretty bride of our Figaro.

MARCELINE: (*with a curtsy*) Secret fiancée of my lord.

SUZANNE: (*with a curtsy*) Who esteems you very much, madam.

MARCELINE: (*with a curtsy*) Will she do me the honor also of loving me a little, madam?

SUZANNE: (*with a curtsy*) As to that, you need have no fears.

MARCELINE: (*with a curtsy*) Madam is so pretty.

SUZANNE: (*with a curtsy*) Why! enough to disconcert madam.

MARCELINE: (*with a curtsy*) Above all, quite respectable.

SUZANNE: (*with a curtsy*) It is up to duennas to be so.

MARCELINE: (*outraged*) Duennas! duennas!

BARTHOLO: (*stopping her*) Marceline!

MARCELINE: Let's go, doctor, I can't restrain myself. Goodbye, madam.   (*A curtsy.*)

SCENE 6

SUZANNE: (*alone*) Go, madam! go, pedant! I fear as little your efforts as I despise your insults.—Look at this old Sibyl! because she has some learning and tormented my lady's youth, she wants to rule the castle. (*She throws her dress from her arm to a chair*) I no longer know what I came for.

SCENE 7

SUZANNE, CHÉRUBIN

CHÉRUBIN: (*running in*) Ah! Suzy, I've been waiting for two hours to catch you alone. Alas! you're getting married and I'm going away.

SUZANNE: How does my marriage cause the departure of my lord's chief page?

CHÉRUBIN: (*piteously*) Suzanne, he has dismissed me.

SUZANNE: (*mimics him*) Chérubin, what! some folly!

CHÉRUBIN: He found me yesterday evening at your cousin Fanchette's. I was rehearsing her small ingenue part for tonight's show, and he flew into a rage on seeing me! "Get out," he said to me, "you little . . ." I don't dare repeat to a woman the bad word he used: "Get out, and tomorrow you won't be at the castle." If my lady, my beautiful godmother doesn't succeed in calming him down, it is all over with me, Suzy. I'll be forever deprived of the happiness of seeing you.

SUZANNE: Of seeing *me*? So it's my turn! You don't go sighing around my lady any more?

CHÉRUBIN: Oh! Suzy. How majestic and beautiful she is, but so imposing!

SUZANNE: That is to say that I am not, and that you can take liberties with me.

CHÉRUBIN: Mean girl, you know only too well I never dare take anything. How lucky you are, seeing her all the time, speaking to her, dressing her in the morning, and undressing her at night, pin by pin . . . oh! Suzy, I'd give anything . . . What is that in your hand?

SUZANNE: (*bantering*) Alas! the blissful bonnet and fortunate ribbon which enclose at night the hair of that beautiful godmother . . .

CHÉRUBIN: (*with animation*) Her ribbon, at night! Give it to me, my love.

SUZANNE: (*pulling it away*) Not so fast! "His love!" How familiar he is! If you were not a brat without importance . . . (CHÉRUBIN *seizes the ribbon*) Ah! the ribbon!

CHÉRUBIN: (*turns around the big armchair*) You can say it is mislaid, ruined, lost; say what you like.

SUZANNE: (*chases after him*) Oh! I promise that in three or four years you will be the biggest little good-for-nothing!

. . . Will you give back that ribbon? (*She wants to take it back.*)

CHÉRUBIN: (*draws a ballad from his pocket*) Let me! ah! do let me have it, Suzy. I'll give you my ballad, and while the memory of your beautiful mistress will sadden all my moments, the memory of you will bring me the only ray of joy that can still divert my heart.

SUZANNE: (*wrests the ballad from his grasp*) Divert your heart, little villain! Do you believe you are talking to your Fanchette? They find you with her, and yet you breathe sighs for my lady; and you make declarations to me into the bargain!

CHÉRUBIN: (*excited*) That is true, on my honor! I no longer know who I am, but just lately I've felt my chest excited; at the mere sight of a woman my heart beats fast; the words "love" and "bliss" make it start and excite it. In short, the need to say to someone "I love you" has become for me so urgent that I say it to myself when I cross the park. I say it to your mistress and to you, to the trees, to the clouds, and to the wind that carries them with my useless words away. Yesterday I met Marceline . . .

SUZANNE: (*laughing*) Ha! ha! ha! ha!

CHÉRUBIN: Why not? She's a woman! she's a maid! A maid! A woman! Oh, what sweet words are those, and how interesting!

SUZANNE: He's becoming crazy!

CHÉRUBIN: Fanchette is sweet, at least she listens to me. You aren't.

SUZANNE: It's quite a pity. Let us listen to the gentleman. (*She wants to snatch the ribbon.*)

CHÉRUBIN: (*turns and flees*) No, no! No one can take it, you see, except with my life. But if the price does not suit you, I'll add to it a thousand kisses. (*He chases her.*)

SUZANNE: (*turns on him as she flees*) A thousand slaps if you come near me. I'm going to complain to my mistress, and far from interceding for you, I myself shall say to my lord: "It serves him right, my lord; chase this little thief, send back to his parents a blackguard who puts on airs about being in love with madam and who on the rebound always wants to kiss me."

CHÉRUBIN: (*sees the* COUNT *enter and hides in fright behind the armchair*) I am lost!

SUZANNE: What a fright!

SCENE 8

SUZANNE, THE COUNT, CHÉRUBIN, *hidden*

SUZANNE: (*sees the* COUNT) Ah! (*She draws near the armchair to conceal* CHÉRUBIN.)

COUNT: (*comes forward*) You are upset, Suzy, you were talking to yourself, and your little heart appears so excited . . . quite understandably on a day like this.

SUZANNE: (*concerned*) My lord, what do you want from me? If someone saw you with me . . .

COUNT: I should be very sorry to be surprised here; but you know the interest I take in you. Bazile must have told you that I love you. I have only a moment to tell you so myself; listen. (*He sits down in the armchair.*)

SUZANNE: (*briskly*) I will listen to nothing.

COUNT: (*takes her hand*) Just one word. You know the King has appointed me ambassador to London. I am taking Figaro with me; I am giving him an excellent position. Now, since it is a wife's duty to follow her husband . . .

SUZANNE: Oh! if I dared speak!

COUNT: (*draws her to him*) Speak, speak, my dear. Take a privilege which you may use with me for life.

SUZANNE: (*frightened*) I don't want to, my lord, I don't want to. Please leave me.

COUNT: But first tell me.

SUZANNE: (*angry*) I don't know any more what I was saying.

COUNT: Something about a wife's duty.

SUZANNE: Very well! when my lord eloped with your lady from the doctor's house and married her for love; when in her honor he abolished a certain dreadful right of the lord of the manor . . .

COUNT: (*gayly*) Which annoyed the girls so much! Ah! Suzy! it was a charming right! And if you'll come and chatter about it this evening in the garden, I shall rate that slight favor so high . . .

BAZILE: (*speaks from outside*) He is not at home, my lord.

COUNT: (*rises*) Whose voice is that?

SUZANNE: How unfortunate I am!

COUNT: Go out so that nobody comes in.

SUZANNE: (*concerned*) And leave you here?

BAZILE: (*exclaims from outside*) My lord was with madam, then he left; I'll go and see.

COUNT: No spot where I can hide! Yes, behind the armchair . . . not very good; but send him away quickly. (SUZANNE *bars his way; he gently pushes her; she retreats and thus comes between him and the little page. But while the* COUNT *stoops and takes* CHÉRUBIN's *place, the latter turns and throws himself kneeling in fright on the chair and curls up.* SUZANNE *takes the dress she was carrying, covers the page with it, and takes her stand in front of the chair.*)

SCENE 9

THE COUNT *and* CHÉRUBIN, *hidden*; SUZANNE, BAZILE

BAZILE: Did you by any chance see my lord, miss?

SUZANNE: (*bluntly*) How could I have seen him? Go away.

BAZILE: (*comes nearer*) If you only thought a little, you would see there was nothing amazing about my question. It's Figaro who is looking for him.

SUZANNE: So he is looking for the man who is his worst enemy after you.

COUNT: (*aside*) Let us see how he takes my side.

BAZILE: To wish a wife well is to wish her husband harm?

SUZANNE: Not in your terrible rules, you vile corrupter.

BAZILE: What does one ask of you that you aren't going to lavish on another? Thanks to a nice ceremony, the things that you were forbidden yesterday will be required of you tomorrow.

SUZANNE: Undeserving wretch!

BAZILE: Marriage being the most comic of serious things, I had thought . . .

SUZANNE: (*indignant*) Disgusting things. Who gave you permission to come in here?

BAZILE: There, there, naughty girl! God calm you! You will do just as you please; but don't believe either that I consider Mr. Figaro the impediment that harms my lord; and if it weren't for the little page . . .

SUZANNE: (*timidly*) Don Chérubin?

BAZILE: (*mimics her*) *Cherubino di amore,*[7] who is always buzzing about you, and who this very morning was prowling here to enter when I left you; say that it isn't true?

SUZANNE: What lies! Go away, evil man!

BAZILE: One is an evil man because one sees through it. Isn't it also for you that the page mysteriously carries a ballad about him?

SUZANNE: Ah! for me indeed! . . .

BAZILE: Unless he composed it for madam! To tell the truth, when he serves at table, they say that he cannot take

[7] *Italian for "cherub of love."*

his eyes off her! . . . But, bless me! let him not play with fire; my lord is a *brute* on that point.

SUZANNE: (*outraged*) And you, quite a villain to go sowing such rumors to ruin a wretched child, who has fallen in his master's disfavor.

BAZILE: Have I invented it? I say it because everybody speaks of it.

COUNT: (*rises*) Who, everybody?

SUZANNE:[8] Ah! Heavens!

BAZILE: Ha! ha!

COUNT: Run along, Bazile, and see that the boy is chased away.

BAZILE: Ah! how sorry I am that I came in here!

SUZANNE: (*agitated*) Dear me! dear me!

COUNT: (*to* BAZILE) She is faint. Help her into this armchair.

SUZANNE: (*repels him energetically*) I don't want to sit down. To enter here without leave is an outrage!

COUNT: We are two with you, my dear. There's no more the least danger!

BAZILE: For my part, I regret having made merry at the page's expense, since you overheard me; I was using it only to ascertain her feelings, because at bottom . . .

COUNT: Fifty pistoles,[9] a horse, and send him back to his parents.

[8] *Beaumarchais's note: "Chérubin in the armchair, the Count, Suzanne, Bazile."*

[9] *The gold pistole is the quarter doubloon of Spain, worth about four dollars.*

BAZILE: My lord, for a trifle?

COUNT: A young libertine whom I found only yesterday with the gardener's daughter.

BAZILE: With Fanchette?

COUNT: And in her room.

SUZANNE: (*indignant*) Where my lord had no doubt business also!

COUNT: (*gayly*) I like that observation.

BAZILE: It is of good omen.

COUNT: (*gayly*) Of course not; I was looking for your uncle Antonio, my drunken gardener, to give him orders. I knock; no one opens for quite a while; your cousin looks confused, I get suspicious, I speak to her, and as I talk I examine. Behind the door there was a sort of curtain, a coatstand, something that covered clothes. Without seeming to, I go softly, softly to lift the curtain (*to illustrate, he lifts the dress off the armchair*), and I see . . . (*He perceives the page.*) Ah! . . .

BAZILE:[10] Ha! ha!

COUNT: This trick is a good one.

BAZILE: Even better.

COUNT: (*to* SUZANNE) Congratulations, miss: scarcely engaged, you make such preparations? Was it to entertain my page that you wished to be alone? And as for you, sir, whose behavior never changes, only the lack of respect for your godmother made you pay your addresses to her chief

[10] *Beaumarchais's note: "Suzanne, Chérubin in the armchair, the Count, Bazile."*

maid, who happens to be your friend's bride! But I will not permit Figaro, a man I esteem and love, to be the victim of such a deception. Was he with you, Bazile?

SUZANNE: (*outraged*) There is neither deception nor victim; he was there while you were talking to me.

COUNT: (*in a temper*) May you lie when you say so! His cruelest enemy would not dare wish him this misfortune.

SUZANNE: He was asking me to beseech madam to obtain his pardon from you. Your arrival upset him so much that he hid in the armchair.

COUNT: (*angry*) Infernal trick! But I sat in that chair when I arrived.

CHÉRUBIN: Alas! my lord, I was shaking behind it.

COUNT: Another deceit! I put myself there just now.

CHÉRUBIN: Pardon me, but that is when I crouched inside.

COUNT: (*more indignant*) Then, this young snake in the grass must be a . . . little serpent! he was listening to us!

CHÉRUBIN: On the contrary, my lord, I did my best to hear nothing.

COUNT: O treachery! (*To* SUZANNE.) You shall not marry Figaro.

BAZILE: Restrain yourself: someone is coming.

COUNT: (*pulling* CHÉRUBIN *out of the armchair and setting him on his feet*) He would stay there before the whole world!

SCENE 10

CHÉRUBIN, SUZANNE, FIGARO, THE COUNTESS,
THE COUNT, FANCHETTE, BAZILE, many valets
and peasants dressed in white

FIGARO: (*holding a woman's toque adorned with white feathers and ribbons, speaks to the* COUNTESS) Only you, madam, can obtain us this favor.

COUNTESS: You see them, Count, they imagine I have an influence which I do not possess. Still, as their request is not unreasonable . . .

COUNT: (*embarrassed*) It would indeed have to be very much so . . .

FIGARO: (*in a low voice to* SUZANNE) Back up my efforts.

SUZANNE: (*in a low voice to* FIGARO) Which will lead to nothing.

FIGARO: (*in a low voice*) Do it anyway.

COUNT: (*to* FIGARO) What do you want?

FIGARO: My lord, your vassals, who are touched by the abolition of a certain troublesome right, which your love for madam . . .

COUNT: Well, this right no longer exists; what do you mean?

FIGARO: (*maliciously*) That it is high time that the virtue of so good a master should manifest itself. It is of such profit to me today that I wish to be the first to glorify it at my wedding.

COUNT: (*more embarrassed*) You can't be serious, my friend. The abolition of a shameful right is only the payment of a debt to respectability. A Spaniard may want to conquer beauty by attention; but to be the first to exact the sweetest of uses as if it were a servile due, ah! that is the tyranny of a Vandal, and not the acknowledged right of a Castilian nobleman.

FIGARO: (*holding* SUZANNE's *hand*) Then permit this young creature, whose honor your wisdom has preserved, to receive publicly from your hand the virginal coif adorned with white feathers and ribbons as a symbol of the purity of your intentions. Adopt this ceremony for all marriages and let an appropriate quatrain be sung in chorus to commemorate the event . . .

COUNT: (*embarrassed*) If I did not know that lover, poet, and musician excuse all sorts of folly . . .

FIGARO: Join with me, my friends.

ALL: (*together*) My lord! my lord!

SUZANNE: (*to the* COUNT) Why shun an honor you so richly deserve?

COUNT: (*aside*) False-hearted wench!

FIGARO: Look at her, my lord, no prettier fiancée will ever signalize the greatness of your sacrifice.

SUZANNE: Leave my face out of it and let us only praise his virtue.

COUNT: (*aside*) This whole thing is a trick.

COUNTESS: I join with them, Count, and this ceremony will always be dear to me, since it owes its being to the gracious love you used to have for me.

COUNT: Which I still have, madam, and because of which I now yield.

ALL: (*together*) Bravo!

COUNT: (*aside*) I'm caught. (*aloud*) So that the ceremony may have a little more splendor, I wish only to see it postponed till somewhat later. (*aside*) Let us get hold quickly of Marceline.

FIGARO: (*to* CHÉRUBIN) Well, my mischievous lad, you're not applauding?

SUZANNE: He is in despair; my lord is sending him away.

COUNTESS: Ah! sir, I ask for his pardon.

COUNT: He doesn't deserve it.

COUNTESS: Alas! he is so young!

COUNT: Not so young as you think.

CHÉRUBIN: (*trembling*) To pardon generously is not the lordly right you gave up when you married madam.

COUNTESS: He only gave up the one that afflicted you all.

SUZANNE: If my lord had abandoned the right to pardon, it would surely be the first one he would like to restore in secret.

COUNT: (*embarrassed*) Yes, no doubt.

COUNTESS: So why restore it?

CHÉRUBIN: (*to the* COUNT) I was fickle in my behavior, my lord, it is true, but never the least impropriety in my words . . .

COUNT: (*embarrassed*) All right, that's enough . . .

FIGARO: What does he mean?

COUNT: (*sharply*) It's enough, it's enough; everybody wants him to be pardoned, I grant it. I'll go further: I'll give him a company in my regiment.

ALL: (*together*) Bravo!

COUNT: But on condition that he leave at once to join up in Catalonia.

FIGARO: Oh! my lord, tomorrow.

COUNT: (*insists*) I order it so.

CHÉRUBIN: I obey.

COUNT: Greet your godmother and beg her protection. (CHÉRUBIN *kneels on one knee before the* COUNTESS, *unable to speak*.)

COUNTESS: (*moved*) Since we can't keep you even for today, young man, go. New duties call you; go and fulfill them worthily. Honor your benefactor. Remember this house where your youth found so much leniency. Be obedient, upright, and brave; we shall share in your success. (CHÉRUBIN *gets up again and goes back to where he stood before*.)

COUNT: You are deeply moved, madam.

COUNTESS: I do not apologize for it. Who knows the lot of a child thrown into such a dangerous career! He is related to my family, and besides he is my godson.

COUNT: (*aside*) I see that Bazile was right. (*aloud*) Young man, kiss Suzanne . . . for the last time.

FIGARO: Why the last, my lord? He'll come and spend

the winter here. Give me a kiss too, captain. (*He embraces him.*) Goodbye, my little Chérubin. You are going to lead quite a different sort of life, my child. Indeed! you will no longer hang about the women's quarters all day; no more canary bread and custard snacks; no more spinning the bottle and blindman's buff. Just good soldiers, by God! tanned, dressed in rags; a huge musket quite heavy. Right turn! Left turn! Forward march! To glory, and don't go stumbling on the way; unless a good shot! . . .

SUZANNE: Horrors! for shame!

COUNTESS: What a prediction!

COUNT: Where can Marceline be? Isn't it queer that she isn't with the rest of you!

FANCHETTE: My lord, she went to town by the lane along the farm.

COUNT: And will she come back?

BAZILE: When it may please God.

FIGARO: If it pleased Him never to please! . . .

FANCHETTE: The doctor was giving her his arm.

COUNT: (*quickly*) The doctor is here?

BAZILE: She grabbed him at once . . .

COUNT: (*aside*) He could not come at a more opportune moment.

FANCHETTE: She looked quite excited; she spoke very loud as she walked, then she would stop and do like this with her arms. And the doctor, he did like this with his hand to calm her down. She seemed so angry! she mentioned my cousin, Figaro.

COUNT: (*takes her chin in his hand*) Future . . . cousin.

FANCHETTE: (*pointing to* CHÉRUBIN) My lord, have you forgiven us for yesterday? . . .

COUNT: (*interrupts*) Good day, good day, my dear.

FIGARO: It's her cursed love that beguiles her;[11] she would have spoiled our party.

COUNT: (*aside*) She will spoil it, I vouch for it. (*aloud*) Come, madam, let us go in. Bazile, you will please stop in to see me.

SUZANNE: (*to* FIGARO) You'll be joining me, sonny?

FIGARO: (*in a low voice to* SUZANNE) Wasn't he properly raked?

SUZANNE: (*in a low voice*) Charming boy! (*Exeunt omnes.*)

SCENE 11

CHÉRUBIN, FIGARO, BAZILE

(*While they go out,* FIGARO *stops them both and brings them back.*)

FIGARO: By the way, you fellows; the ceremony having been adopted, tonight's show becomes the sequel. We must rehearse our parts; let's not do like those players who never act so badly as on the day when critics are wide awake. We

[11] *The allusion is to Marceline.*

haven't any tomorrow to excuse us. So let's learn our parts well today.

BAZILE: (*maliciously*) Mine is harder than you think.

FIGARO: (*making, without* BAZILE's *seeing him, the gesture of thrashing him*) You don't suspect also the ovation you will get.

CHÉRUBIN: Dear friend, you forget that I am leaving.

FIGARO: And you, you would rather stay!

CHÉRUBIN: Oh, if I only could!

FIGARO: Then, we must use craft. Not a murmur at your leaving. Traveling cloak on your shoulders; do your packing so that everyone can see; your horse at the gates; a little gallop up to the farm; come back on foot by the back way. My lord will believe you gone: just keep out of his sight; I undertake to calm him after the show.

CHÉRUBIN: But there's Fanchette who doesn't know her role!

BAZILE: What the deuce have you been teaching her for the past week when you haven't been away from her?

FIGARO: You have nothing to do today; please coach her in her lines.

BAZILE: Be careful, young man, be careful! Her father is not satisfied; the girl has been slapped and hasn't learned her lines. Chérubin! Chérubin! you will cause her sorrow! *The pot goes too often to the well!* . . .

FIGARO: Ah! there's our fossil with his old proverbs. Well, you old pedant! What does the wisdom of nations have to say? *The pot goes so often to the well that at last . . .*

BAZILE: *It gets filled.*[12]

FIGARO: (*going away*) Not so dumb, however, not so dumb.

---

[12] *Bazile's penchant for changing old proverbs is referred to in* The Barber of Seville: *see* ACT IV, SCENE I.

ACT TWO

The stage represents a superb bedroom, a large bed in an alcove, a platform in front. The main door is upstage to the right, the dressing-room door is downstage to the left. Another door, at the rear, leads to the women's quarters. A window opens on the opposite side.

SCENE I

SUZANNE, THE COUNTESS, *enter by the right door*

COUNTESS: (*throws herself into an easy chair*) Shut the door, Suzanne, and tell me everything in the greatest detail.

SUZANNE: I didn't hold back anything, madam.

COUNTESS: So, Suzy, he wanted to seduce you?

SUZANNE: Oh no! My lord does not take that much trouble with a servant; he wanted to buy me.

COUNTESS: And the little page was there?

SUZANNE: That is to say, he was hidden behind the big armchair. He had come to beg me to intercede with you for his pardon.

COUNTESS: Why not direct himself to me? would I have refused him?

SUZANNE: That's what I told him, but his regrets at leaving, especially at leaving you! "Ah!" he said, "Suzy, how noble and beautiful she is! but how imposing!"

COUNTESS: Do I really look that way, Suzy, I who have always protected him?

SUZANNE: Then he saw the ribbon of your nightdress which I held in my hand, and he jumped upon it . . .

COUNTESS: (*smiling*) My ribbon? . . . What a child!

SUZANNE: I tried to take it from him, madam, but he was like a lion, his eyes were shining . . . "You'll get it only with my life," he said in his little voice, gentle and high-pitched.

COUNTESS: (*dreaming*) Well, Suzy?

SUZANNE: Well, madam, can one put an end to that little demon? My godmother one moment; I would be willing to add "the next." And because he wouldn't even dare to kiss the hem of your dress, madam, he always wishes to kiss me.

COUNTESS: (*dreaming*) Enough . . . enough of this idle talk . . . At last, my poor Suzanne, my husband finally told you?

SUZANNE: That if I refused to listen to him, he was going to use his influence in behalf of Marceline.

COUNTESS: (*gets up, paces, and uses her fan vigorously*) He does not love me at all any more.

SUZANNE: Why so much jealousy on his part?

COUNTESS: Like all husbands, my dear! solely through pride. I loved him too much: I wearied him with my caresses and bored him with my love: that was my only wrong with him. But I do not intend that this just confession should bring you any harm, and you shall marry Figaro. He alone can help us: is he coming?

SUZANNE: As soon as he sees the hunt leave.

COUNTESS: (*using her fan*) Open the window on the garden a little. It's very warm here! . . .

SUZANNE: It's because madam has been talking and walking actively. (*She goes to open the window at the rear.*)

COUNTESS: (*dreaming a long time*) If it weren't for this set purpose in avoiding me . . . Men are guilty creatures!

SUZANNE: (*shouts from the window*) Ah! there is my lord riding through the big garden, followed by Pédrille and two, three, four greyhounds.

COUNTESS: We have plenty of time. (*She sits down.*) Someone is knocking, Suzy.

SUZANNE: (*runs singing to the door*) Why, it's my Figaro, it's my Figaro!

SCENE 2

FIGARO, SUZANNE, THE COUNTESS, *sitting*

SUZANNE: My dear friend, come in! Madam is so impatient to see you! . . .

FIGARO: And how about you, my little Suzanne? Madam must not take on so. After all, what is it about? a trifle. My lord, the Count, finds our young lady lovable and would like to make her his mistress, it's quite natural.

SUZANNE: Natural?

FIGARO: Then he appointed me King's messenger and Suzy attachée to the Embassy. There's no oversight there.

SUZANNE: Are you through?

FIGARO: And because Suzanne, my fiancée, declines the post and its privileges, he is going to favor Marceline's plans. What could be more simple? To avenge oneself on those who harm our plans by upsetting theirs is what everybody does, it's what we ourselves are going to do. And that is all in a nutshell.

COUNTESS: Figaro, can you treat so lightly a project that will cost us all our happiness?

FIGARO: Who says it will, madam?

SUZANNE: Instead of sharing our grief . . .

FIGARO: Isn't it enough that I busy myself with it? Now, to act as methodically as he, let us first moderate his great desire for our belongings in arousing in him a fear for his own.

COUNTESS: It's a good idea, but how?

FIGARO: It's already done, madam; a false information given about you . . .

COUNTESS: About me! you are out of your mind!

FIGARO: Oh! it is he who must lose his.

COUNTESS: A man jealous like him! . . .

FIGARO: So much the better; to take advantage of people like him, one must whip up their blood a little; a device women understand so well! Then, as soon as men of his type are red hot with anger, a bit of intrigue enables one to lead them by the nose into the Guadalquivir.[1] I have made Bazile deliver an anonymous note which warns my lord that tonight a gallant will try to see you during the ball.

COUNTESS: And so you made game of the truth when it concerns a woman of honor?

FIGARO: There are few, madam, that I would have dared to risk it with, for fear of hitting the mark.

COUNTESS: And now I'll have to thank him!

FIGARO: But tell me whether it isn't delightful to have cut out his work for him so that he'll spend prowling, swearing around his lady the time he counted on for taking pleasure with ours! Already he is quite confused: will he gallop over this one? will he keep watch over that one? In his disturbed state of mind, look, look, there he is racing across the meadow after a hare at the end of his tether. The hour of the wedding hastens on, he cannot have made a decision against it, and never will he dare oppose it to madam's face.

SUZANNE: No, but Marceline, that great mind, will venture to do it.

FIGARO: Brrrr! That worries me a lot, indeed! Let my lord know that you will go at dusk to the garden.

SUZANNE: You rely on him?

---

[1] *The Guadalquivir is a Spanish river about 350 miles long. Its source is in the Sierra de Cazorla, and it flows in Andalusia.*

FIGARO: Oh! well! listen to me: people who don't want to do anything about anything do not achieve anything and are not good for anything. That's my motto.

SUZANNE: A nice one!

COUNTESS: Like this idea of hers. You would really let her go?

FIGARO: Not at all. I'll have someone put on one of Suzanne's dresses. Seized in the act, can the Count deny it?

SUZANNE: Who will wear my dress?

FIGARO: Chérubin.

COUNTESS: He's left.

FIGARO: Not according to me. Will you leave me alone?

SUZANNE: One can always trust him to hatch a scheme.

FIGARO: Two, three, four at once, quite tangled, crossing each other. I was born to be a courtier.

SUZANNE: They say it's a hard profession!

FIGARO: Receive, take, and ask: there's the secret in three words.

COUNTESS: He has so much self-confidence that it finally rubs off on me.

FIGARO: That was my scheme.

SUZANNE: You were saying? . . .

FIGARO: That during my lord's absence I'm going to send you Chérubin; do his hair, dress him, I'll hide and indoctrinate him. And after that dance, my lord. (*Exit.*)

SCENE 3

SUZANNE, THE COUNTESS, *sitting*

COUNTESS: (*holding her box of patches*) Dear me, Suzy, I look a mess! . . . this young man is coming in! . . .

SUZANNE: Don't you want him to escape?

COUNTESS: (*dreams before her small mirror*) I? . . . you'll see how I'm going to scold him.

SUZANNE: Let's get him to sing his ballad. (*She lays it on the* COUNTESS's *lap.*)

COUNTESS: But . . . truly my hair is in such a state! . . .

SUZANNE: (*laughing*) I have only to roll up the two curls, madam will scold him much better.

COUNTESS: (*coming back to herself*) What are you saying, miss?

SCENE 4

CHÉRUBIN, *with a look of shame;* SUZANNE; THE COUNTESS, *sitting*

SUZANNE: Come in, officer; we are presentable.

CHÉRUBIN: (*comes forward trembling*) Oh! how that

title affects me, madam! It tells me that I must leave a place . . . a godmother . . . so good to me! . . .

SUZANNE: And so beautiful!

CHÉRUBIN: (*with a sigh*) Oh, yes!

SUZANNE: (*mimics him*) "Oh, yes!" The good young man, with his long, hypocritical lashes. Come, fine blue-bird, sing a ballad for madam.

COUNTESS: (*unfolds the paper*) Whose do they say it is?

SUZANNE: See the blush of the guilty one; it's a foot deep on his cheeks.

CHÉRUBIN: Is it forbidden . . . to cherish . . . ?

SUZANNE: (*shakes her fist in his face*) I'll tell all, good-for-nothing!

COUNTESS: Enough . . . does he sing?

CHÉRUBIN: Oh! madam, I'm trembling all over! . . .

SUZANNE: (*laughing*) And nya, nya, nya, nya, nya, nya, nya. As soon as madam wishes, modest author! I'm going to accompany him.

COUNTESS: Take my guitar. (*The* COUNTESS, *sitting, holds the paper to follow the words.* SUZANNE, *behind her armchair, begins the introduction, reading the notes over her mistress's head. The little page stands before her, his eyes lowered. The scene duplicates the fine print after Vanloo, entitled* CONVERSATION IN SPAIN.[2])

[2] *Beaumarchais's note: Chérubin, the Countess, Suzanne.*

BALLAD

Tune: *Marlbrough s'en va-t-en guerre*[3]

FIRST COUPLET

My charger's out of breath
(How my heart, how my heart is breaking!)
I went from plain to plain
At the will of my steed.

SECOND COUPLET

At the will of my steed,
Without varlet or squire;
There,[4] close to a fountain,
(How my heart, how my heart is breaking!)
Thinking of my godmother,
I felt my tears flowing.

THIRD COUPLET

I felt my tears flowing,
Ready was I to grieve;
I climbed upon an ash tree,
(How my heart, how my heart is breaking!)
Her letter without mine;
The king happened to pass.

FOURTH COUPLET

The king happened to pass,
His barons, his clergy.
"Handsome page," said the Queen,

---

[3] *The tune given makes a literal translation almost possible. The poem is not good.*

[4] *Beaumarchais's note: At the performance of the play, they began the ballad with this line saying:* Auprès d'une fontaine.

(How my heart, how my heart is breaking!)
  Who puts you in such distress
  That draws from you such tears?

FIFTH COUPLET

  Who draws from you such tears?
  You must tell us, poor lad."
  "My Queen, my lady fair,
(How my heart, how my heart is breaking!)
  A godmother had I
  Whom always I adored.[5]

SIXTH COUPLET

  Whom always I adored;
  I think I shall die of it."
  "Handsome page," said the Queen,
(How my heart, how my heart is breaking!)
  "A godmother only is she;
  Pray, let me take her place.

SEVENTH COUPLET

  Pray, let me take her place;
  I shall make you my page,
  Then to my young Helen fair,
(How my heart, how my heart is breaking!)
  A captain's daughter true,
  To whom I'll marry you.

EIGHTH COUPLET

  To whom I'll marry you.
  No, I must not speak a word,
  I want, dragging my chain,

[5] *Beaumarchais's note: Here the Countess stops the page by closing the paper. The remainder is not sung on the stage.*

(How my heart, how my heart is breaking!)
 To die of this distress,
 But not console myself."

COUNTESS: It is full of simplicity . . . , even of true sentiment.

SUZANNE: (*goes and lays the guitar on a chair*)[6] Oh! as far as sentiment is concerned, he's a young man who . . . But say, officer, has one told you that, to enliven the evening, we want to know beforehand whether one of my gowns will more or less fit you?

COUNTESS: I am afraid not.

SUZANNE: (*compares their statures*) He is about my size. Let's take off the cloak. (*She takes it off him.*)

COUNTESS: And suppose someone should come in?

SUZANNE: Are we doing anything wrong? I'm going to shut the door. (*She runs.*) But it's the hair I want to see.

COUNTESS: In my dressing room, a bathrobe. (SUZANNE *goes into the dressing room, the door of which is at the edge of the stage.*)

SCENE 5

CHÉRUBIN, THE COUNTESS, *seated*

COUNTESS: Until the ball is initiated, the Count will not know that you are still in the castle. We shall tell him

[6] *Beaumarchais's note: Chérubin, Suzanne, the Countess.*

afterwards that the time to send your commission gave us the idea of . . .

CHÉRUBIN: (*shows it to her*) Alas! madam, it is here; Bazile handed it to me from my lord.

COUNTESS: Already? They feared they were going to lose a minute's time. (*She reads.*) They were in so much of a hurry that they forgot to affix the seal. (*She hands it back to him.*)

SCENE 6

CHÉRUBIN, THE COUNTESS, SUZANNE

SUZANNE: (*enters with a large hat*) The seal to what?

COUNTESS: To his commission.

SUZANNE: Already?

COUNTESS: It's what I was saying. Is that my bathrobe?

SUZANNE: (*sits near the* COUNTESS)[7] And the most handsome of all. (*She sings with pins in her mouth.*)

> Turn your head, Johnny of Lyra,
> Turn your head, my handsome friend.

(CHÉRUBIN *kneels beside her. She dresses his hair.*) Madam, he is so charming!

COUNTESS: Pull his collar so that it is a little more like a woman's.

SUZANNE: (*adjusts it*) There . . . Look at that brat,

[7] *Beaumarchais's note: Chérubin, Suzanne, the Countess.*

what a pretty girl he makes! I am jealous! (*She takes his chin.*) Will you be not so pretty as you are!

COUNTESS: She's crazy! You must turn back the cuff so that the undersleeve shows up better . . . (*She turns back the cuff*) What has he on his arm? A ribbon!

SUZANNE: Your ribbon. I am glad madam saw it. I had warned him that I would tell on him. Oh! if my lord had not come, I would certainly have gotten the ribbon back, for I'm nearly as strong as he.

COUNTESS: There is blood. (*She takes off the ribbon.*)

CHÉRUBIN: (*sheepish*) This morning, when I knew I had to leave, I was adjusting the curb of my horse; it tossed its head and the boss on the bit grazed my arm.

COUNTESS: Why one has never put a ribbon . . .

SUZANNE: A stolen ribbon at that!—Just imagine what the boss bit . . . the curb bit . . . the cornet of the horse . . .[8] I don't understand a thing about those names. —Just look at that white skin! It's a woman's arm, whiter than mine! See, madam. (*She compares them.*)

COUNTESS: (*frigidly*) Get me rather some court plaster from my dressing table. (SUZANNE *shoves* CHÉRUBIN's *head laughing, he falls forward on his hands. She goes into the dressing room at the edge of the stage.*)

---

[8] *The horse has no* cornette. *Beaumarchais wants the*—ette *effect, conveyed by* bossette, courbette, *and* cornette, *which cannot be rendered in English. Obviously, Suzanne does not know the parts of a horse's trappings.*

SCENE 7

CHÉRUBIN, *kneeling*; THE COUNTESS, *sitting*

COUNTESS: (*remains a moment without talking, her eyes on her ribbon.* CHÉRUBIN *looks at her intently*) As for my ribbon, sir, . . . as it is the one whose color most suits me . . . I was very angry to be without it.

SCENE 8

CHÉRUBIN, *kneeling*; THE COUNTESS,
sitting; SUZANNE

SUZANNE: (*coming back*) And the bandage for his arm? (*She hands to the* COUNTESS *the plaster and a pair of scissors.*)

COUNTESS: When you go for your clothes, bring back the ribbon from another bonnet. (SUZANNE *leaves by the main door, taking the page's cloak with her.*)

SCENE 9

CHÉRUBIN, *kneeling;* THE COUNTESS, *sitting*

CHÉRUBIN: (*his eyes lowered*) That which you're taking from me would have cured me in no time.

COUNTESS: Owing to what virtue? (*Pointing to the plaster.*) This is better.

CHÉRUBIN: (*hesitating*) When a ribbon . . . has bound the head . . . or touched the skin of a person . . .

COUNTESS: (*breaking in*) . . . of a stranger, is it good for wounds? I did not know this property. To test it, I'll keep this one, which you put around your arm. At the first scratch . . . on one of my maids, I'll try it out.

CHÉRUBIN: (*full of conviction*) You are keeping it and I'm leaving.

COUNTESS: Not forever.

CHÉRUBIN: I'm so unhappy!

COUNTESS: (*moved*) Now he is weeping! It's that awful Figaro with his prediction!

CHÉRUBIN: (*excited*) Oh! I wish the time of his prediction had come! Sure of dying at once, perhaps my lips would dare . . .

COUNTESS: (*interrupts him and wipes his eyes with her handkerchief*) Be quiet, child, be quiet. There isn't a grain of sense in all you're saying. (*Someone knocks at the door; she raises her voice.*) Who is it?

SCENE 10

CHÉRUBIN, THE COUNTESS; THE COUNT, *outside*

COUNT: (*outside*) Why are you locked in?

COUNTESS: (*upset, gets up*) It's my husband! Great Heavens! . . . (*To* CHÉRUBIN, *who has also risen.*) You without your cloak, your collar and your arms bare! alone with me! this disarray, an anonymous letter received, his jealousy! . . .

COUNT: (*outside*) You won't open?

COUNTESS: It's because . . . I'm alone . . .

COUNT: (*outside*) Alone! With whom were you talking, then?

COUNTESS: (*fumbling*) . . . With you, no doubt.

CHÉRUBIN: (*aside*) After the scenes of yesterday and this morning, he would kill me on the spot! (*He runs into the dressing room and slams the door.*)

SCENE 11

COUNTESS: (*alone, removes the key and opens the other door to admit the* COUNT) Ah! what a mistake, what a mistake!

SCENE 12

THE COUNT, THE COUNTESS

COUNT: (*a little severe*) You are not in the habit of shutting yourself up!

COUNTESS: (*agitated*) I . . . I was trying on . . . Yes, odds and ends with Suzanne, she went into her room for a minute.

COUNT: (*scrutinizes her*) You look and sound quite strange.

COUNTESS: It's not astonishing . . . not astonishing at all . . . I assure you . . . We were speaking about you . . . She went, as I told you.

COUNT: You were speaking about me! . . . I have come back much disturbed. On setting out, I was handed a note, which I do not believe in, nevertheless it has disturbed me.

COUNTESS: How, sir? . . . what note?

COUNT: You must admit, madam, that you or I am surrounded by creatures who are . . . quite wicked! Someone informs me that some time today a person whom I suppose to be absent, will seek to talk to you.

COUNTESS: Whoever this rash being may be, he will have to enter this very spot; for my intention is not to stir from this room for the rest of the day.

COUNT: What about this evening, for Suzanne's wedding?

COUNTESS: Not at any price; I am quite indisposed.

COUNT: Luckily the doctor is here. (*The page overturns a chair in the dressing-room.*) What was that noise?

COUNTESS: (*more agitated*) Noise?

COUNT: Someone overturned a piece of furniture.

COUNTESS: I . . . I heard nothing.

COUNT: You must be greatly preoccupied!

COUNTESS: Preoccupied! what about?

COUNT: Madam, there is someone in that room.

COUNTESS: Indeed, who can there be, sir?

COUNT: I ask that question; I have just arrived.

COUNTESS: But . . . it must be Suzanne putting things away.

COUNT: You said she had gone to her room!

COUNTESS: Gone there . . . or here, I don't know which.

COUNT: If it is Suzanne, how is it you are so distressed?

COUNTESS: Distressed over my maid?

COUNT: I don't know whether it is over your maid; but it is distress, assuredly.

COUNTESS: Assuredly, sir, that girl disturbs and occupies your mind much more than I.

COUNT: (*angry*) She occupies my mind to such an extent, madam, that I want to see her at once.

COUNTESS: I certainly believe that this is what you often want. But you have very ill-founded suspicions . . .

SCENE 13

THE COUNT, THE COUNTESS; SUZANNE *enters*
with clothes in her arms and pushes the rear door

COUNT: Therefore, they will be easier to dispel. (*He speaks through the dressing-room door.*) Come out, Suzy, I order you to. (SUZANNE *stops near the alcove in the rear.*)

COUNTESS: She is nearly naked, sir. Does one intrude in this way on women in their apartments? She was trying on some clothes I am giving her for her wedding; she fled when she heard you.

COUNT: If she fears so much to show herself, she can at least talk. (*He turns to the closed door.*) Answer me, Suzanne, are you in the dressing-room? (SUZANNE, *still in the rear, jumps into the alcove, and hides.*)

COUNTESS: (*quickly, to the closed door*) Suzy, I forbid you to answer. (*To the* COUNT.) One has never carried tyranny so far!

COUNT: (*advances toward the dressing-room*) Oh well! since she won't speak, dressed or undressed, I shall see her.

COUNTESS: (*intercepts him*) Anywhere else I cannot prevent it; but I hope that in my own room . . .

COUNT: And I hope that in one minute I shall know who this mysterious Suzanne is. To ask you for the key, I see would be useless; but there is a way to break down this flimsy door. Ho there, somebody!

COUNTESS: Bring in your people, create a public scandal of a suspicion that would make us the talk of the castle?

COUNT: A good point, madam, I alone can do it; I'm going at once to my room to take what I need . . . (*He starts to go and comes back.*) But in order that everything should remain in the same place, will you kindly accompany me, decently and noiselessly since scandal displeases you so? . . . A request so simple will apparently not be denied!

COUNTESS: (*upset*) Why, sir, who would dream of opposing you?

COUNT: Ah! I was forgetting the door that leads to your maid's quarters; I must also shut it in order that you may be fully vindicated. (*He goes to close the rear center door and he takes away the key.*)

COUNTESS: (*aside*) Oh Heaven! what a fatal oversight!

COUNT: (*returning to her*) Now that this room is locked, I beg you to accept my arm; (*he raises his voice*) and, as for Suzanne in the dressing-room, she will have to have the goodness to wait for me, and the least evil that can happen to her on my return is . . .

COUNTESS: Truly, sir, this is the most odious performance . . . (*The* COUNT *leads her out and locks the door.*)

SCENE 14

SUZANNE, CHÉRUBIN

SUZANNE: (*comes out of the alcove, runs to the dressing-room, and speaks through the keyhole*) Open up, Chérubin, open quickly, it's Suzanne; open and hurry out.

CHÉRUBIN: (*comes out*)[9] Oh! Suzanne, what a dreadful mess!

SUZANNE: Go, you haven't a minute to lose.

CHÉRUBIN: (*frightened*) But how can I get out?

SUZANNE: I don't know, just go.

CHÉRUBIN: But there is no way out?

SUZANNE: After the encounter of a little while ago, he would crush you! and we'd[10] be doomed. Go tell Figaro . . .

CHÉRUBIN: Maybe the window over the garden is not very high up. (*He runs to look.*)

SUZANNE: (*frightened*) A whole story! impossible! Oh my poor lady! And my marriage, o Heaven!

CHÉRUBIN: (*comes back*) It overlooks the melon-patch; all it can spoil is a bed or two . . .

SUZANNNE: (*holds him back and exclaims*) He is going to kill himself!

[9] *Beaumarchais's note: Chérubin, Suzanne.*
[10] *The es of* perdues *makes it clear that the Countess and Suzanne are meant by the "we."*

CHÉRUBIN: (*excited*) In an open furnace I would throw myself, Suzy, rather than cause her any harm. And this kiss will bring me luck. (*He kisses her, runs toward the window, and leaps out.*)

SCENE 15

SUZANNE: (*alone; a cry of terror*) Ah! (*Overcome, she falls into a chair for a moment. She drags herself to the window and comes back.*) He's already far. Oh! the little scamp! as nimble on his feet as pretty to look at! If he wants for women . . . Let us take his place as soon as possible. (*Going into the dressing-room.*) Now you can, my lord, tear down the wall if it delights you, you don't get a word out of me! (*She shuts herself in.*)

SCENE 16

THE COUNT, THE COUNTESS, *return to the room*

COUNT: (*in his hand a pair of pliers, which he throws upon the armchair*) Everything is certainly as I left it. Madam, if I'm compelled to break down that door, reflect on the consequences: once again, will you open it yourself?

COUNTESS: But sir, what horrible mood can so change considerateness between husband and wife? If love possessed you to the point of inspiring this fury, I could excuse it, despite its lack of reason. I would forget because of the motive, the offense. But how can vanity alone move a well-bred man to such excesses?

COUNT: Love or vanity, you shall open the door, or I'm going at once . . .

COUNTESS: (*before the* COUNT) Please desist, sir. Do you believe me capable of forgetting what I owe my self-respect?

COUNT: Anything you please, madam, but I will see who is in that room.

COUNTESS: (*frightened*) Very well, sir, you shall see. Listen to me . . . calmly.

COUNT: So it isn't Suzanne.

COUNTESS: (*timidly*) At least it isn't a person either . . . about whom you should have any fear . . . We were arranging a practical joke . . . quite harmless, really, for this evening . . . and I swear to you . . .

COUNT: And you swear to me?

COUNTESS: That neither one[11] nor the other had a mind to offend you.

COUNT: (*quickly*) Neither one nor the other? it's a man.

COUNTESS: A child, sir.

COUNT: And who?

COUNTESS: I scarcely dare give his name.

COUNT: (*furious*) I'll kill him.

COUNTESS: Merciful Heavens!

[11] *The French* l'un que l'autre *makes it clear that a man is involved. One could not tell from the English equivalent.*

COUNT: Then speak up.

COUNTESS: That young . . . Chérubin . . .

COUNT: Chérubin! The insolent whelp! That explains my suspicions and the note.

COUNTESS: (*joining her hands in prayer*) Oh! sir, take care not to think . . .

COUNT: (*stamping his foot*) (*aside*) I find that cursed page wherever I go. (*aloud*) Come, madam, open up; now I know everything. You would not have been moved in taking your leave of him this morning; he would have left when I ordered it; you would not have used such lies in your tale of Suzanne; he would not have hidden himself so carefully unless there was something criminal about it.

COUNTESS: He was afraid of irritating you by showing himself.

COUNT: (*beside himself, shouting at the dressing-room door*) Come out, you little wretch!

COUNTESS: (*seizes him with both arms and thrusts him away*) Ah! sir, sir, your anger makes me tremble for him. Please do not believe an unjust suspicion and don't let the disorder you'll find him in . . .

COUNT: Disorder!

COUNTESS: Alas! yes. He was ready to dress as a woman, one of my bonnets on his head, a jacket without a cloak, his neckband open, his arms bare. He was going to try to . . .

COUNT: And you wanted to stay in your room! Unworthy wife! You shall keep to your room . . . a long time; but first I must kick out that insolent child so as not to run into him anywhere else.

COUNTESS: (*on her knees, arms uplifted*) Count, spare a mere child; I should never forgive myself for having caused . . .

COUNT: Your fears aggravate his crime.

COUNTESS: He is not guilty, he was leaving. It is I who had him called back.

COUNT: (*furious*) Get up. Remove yourself . . . You are quite bold to dare speak to me in behalf of another!

COUNTESS: Very well! I will remove myself, sir, I will get up, I will even deliver to you the key to the door; but, in the name of your love . . .

COUNT: My love! False-hearted one!

COUNTESS: (*gets up and gives him the key*) Promise me you will let that child go without doing him any harm, and afterwards may you vent all your anger on me, if I do not convince you . . .

COUNT: (*taking the key*) I am no longer listening.

COUNTESS: (*throws herself into an easy chair, her hand-kerchief over her eyes*) O Heaven! he's going to die!

COUNT: (*opens the door and retreats*) It's Suzanne!

SCENE 17

THE COUNT, THE COUNTESS, SUZANNE

SUZANNE: (*comes out laughing*) "I'll kill him! I'll kill him!" Why don't you kill him, that wicked page?

COUNT: (*aside*) Oh! what a lesson! (*Looking at the* COUNTESS, *who is stupefied.*) And you pretend to be astonished, too? . . . But maybe she was not alone. (*He goes in.*)

SCENE 18

THE COUNTESS, *sitting;* SUZANNE

SUZANNE (*hastens to her mistress*) Recover, madam, he is quite far; he jumped . . .

COUNTESS: Oh! Suzy, I am all in.

SCENE 19

THE COUNTESS, *sitting;* SUZANNE, THE COUNT

COUNT: (*emerges from the dressing-room baffled. After a brief silence.*) There is no one and this time I was wrong. —Madam, . . . you are a good actress.

SUZANNE: *(gayly)* How about me, my lord? *(The* COUNTESS, *her handkerchief on her mouth, does not speak, to regain her composure.)*

COUNT: *(approaches)*[12] What, madam, you were joking?

COUNTESS: *(recovering a little)* And why not, sir?

COUNT: What a horrible joke! and for what reason, I beg of you? . . .

COUNTESS: Do your outrages deserve any consideration?

COUNT: Do you call outrages what relates to honor!

COUNTESS: *(gradually herself again)* Did I marry you only to be the perpetual victim of neglect and jealousy, which only you dare reconcile?

COUNT: Ah! Madam, you don't spare me.

SUZANNE: Madam had only to let you call the servants.

COUNT: You are right and it's up to me to abase myself . . . Forgive me. I am so confused! . . .

SUZANNE: Admit, my lord, that you deserve to be a bit so.

COUNT: But why didn't you come out when I called you? Naughty girl!

SUZANNE: I was putting on some clothes as best I could, with a multitude of pins, and madam's forbidding me to stir was for a good reason.

COUNT: Instead of reminding me of my error, help me to soothe her.

COUNTESS: No, sir; such an outrage cannot be extenuated. I am going to the Ursulines[13] and it's time I did.

[12] Beaumarchais's note: Suzanne, the Countess sitting, the Count.
[13] The Ursulines are nuns. The order was founded in 1537 in Brescia by Saint Angela Merici (1511-40).

COUNT: Could you do it without some regrets?

SUZANNE: For my part, I am sure that the day of departure will be the beginning of tears.

COUNTESS: And even if that were the case, Suzy, I'd rather miss him than have the baseness to forgive him. He has wounded me too deeply.

COUNT: Rosine!

COUNTESS: I am no longer that Rosine whom you pursued so much! I am the Countess Almaviva, the sad forsaken wife whom you no longer love.

SUZANNE: Oh, madam . . .

COUNT: (*entreating*). For pity's sake . . .

COUNTESS: You never showed me any.

COUNT: But that note . . . It curdled my blood!

COUNTESS: I had not agreed to its being written.

COUNT: You knew about it?

COUNTESS: It was that scatter-brained Figaro . . .

COUNT: He was in on it?

COUNTESS: . . . who handed it to Bazile.

COUNT: . . . who told me he got it from a peasant. Oh false-hearted singing-teacher! two-faced underling! you shall pay for everyone.

COUNTESS: You beg for yourself a forgiveness that you deny to others: how like a man! Ah! if ever I consented to pardon you for the error you committed on the strength of that note, I should demand that the amnesty be general.

COUNT: Very well, with all my heart, Countess. But how can I make amends for so humiliating a mistake?

COUNTESS: (*rises*) It was humiliating for both of us.

COUNT: No, say for me alone. But I am still astonished at the ease with which women take on the proper look and tone of circumstances. You were blushing, weeping, your face was drawn . . . 'Pon my honor, you still look that way.

COUNTESS: (*forcing herself to smile*) I was red . . . with resentment against your suspicions. But are men delicate enough to distinguish the indignation of an honorable creature suffering outrage from the confusion created by a justified accusation?

COUNT: (*smiling*) What about that disheveled page, in his short jacket and half-naked? . . .

COUNTESS: (*pointing to* SUZANNE) You see him before you. Don't you prefer finding this one to the other? Generally speaking, you do not hate to catch this one.

COUNT: (*laughing more vigorously*) And those entreaties, those feigned tears . . .

COUNTESS: You make me laugh and I feel little like it.

COUNT: We men think we are worth something in the art of politics, but we are mere children. It is you, madam, whom the King should send as ambassador to London! Your sex must have made a very deep study of the art of self-control to succeed to this extent!

COUNTESS: We are forced into it always by men.

SUZANNE: Put us, your prisoners, on parole and you will see whether we are honorable creatures.

COUNTESS: Let's break it off, Count. Perhaps I went too

far, but my leniency in so grave a case must at least obtain for me yours.

COUNT: Please repeat that you forgive me.

COUNTESS: Have I said it, Suzy?

SUZANNE: I did not hear it, madam.

COUNT: Very well, let that word slip out.

COUNTESS: You deserve it, then, ingrate?

COUNT: Yes, by my repentance.

SUZANNE: To suspect a man in madam's dressing-room!

COUNT: She has punished me so severely!

SUZANNE: Not to trust her when she says it is her chambermaid!

COUNT: Rosine, are you so merciless?

COUNTESS: Oh! Suzy, how weak I am! what an example I set for you! (*Holding out her hand to the* COUNT.) No one will ever believe again in a woman's anger.

SUZANNE: All right, madam. Mustn't one always come to this with men? (*The* COUNT *ardently kisses his wife's hand.*)

SCENE 20

SUZANNE, FIGARO, THE COUNTESS, THE COUNT

FIGARO: (*arriving out of breath*) They said that madam was indisposed. I ran quickly . . . I see joyfully that there is no truth to the report.

COUNT: (*drily*) You are very attentive!

FIGARO: It's my duty. But there is nothing in it, my lord, all your young vassals of both sexes are downstairs with their violins and bagpipes, waiting to accompany me the moment when you will allow me to bring my fiancée . . .

COUNT: And who will look after the Countess at the castle?

FIGARO: Look after her? She's not sick.

COUNT: No, but there is an absent stranger who must talk to her?

FIGARO: What stranger?

COUNT: The man in the note you handed to Bazile.

FIGARO: Who said that?

COUNT: Even if I hadn't been told, scoundrel! your lying face would prove it to me.

FIGARO: So it's my face that's lying, not I.

SUZANNE: My poor Figaro, don't waste your eloquence in defeat: we have told everything.

FIGARO: Told what? You treat me like a Bazile!

SUZANNE: That you had written the note referred to in order to make my lord believe that when he came in, the young page would be in this dressing-room where I shut myself up.

COUNT: What have you to say to that?

COUNTESS: There's nothing further to hide, Figaro, the joke is over.

FIGARO: *(trying to guess)* The joke . . . is over?

COUNT: Yes, over, consummated. What do you say to that?

FIGARO: I say . . . that I wish I could say as much for my marriage, and if you give the word . . .

COUNT: So you admit the note?

FIGARO: Since madam wants it so, Suzanne wants it so, and you yourself want it so, I must certainly want it so too. But if I were you, my lord, truly, I wouldn't believe a word of anything we are telling you.

COUNT: You're always telling lies in the face of evidence! In short, it's getting on my nerves!

COUNTESS: (*laughing*) The poor fellow! Why do you expect him, sir, to tell the truth even once?

FIGARO: (*in a low voice to* SUZANNE) I have warned him of his danger; that's all a gentleman can do.

SUZANNE: (*in a low voice*) Did you see the little page?

FIGARO: (*in a low voice*) Still all bruised.

SUZANNE: (*in a low voice*) Oh, what a pity!

COUNTESS: Come, Count, they long to be united; their impatience is natural; let us go in for the ceremony.

COUNT: (*aside*) But Marceline, Marceline . . . (*aloud*) I wish to be . . . at least dressed.

COUNTESS: For our own people! Am I dressed?

SCENE 21

FIGARO, SUZANNE, THE COUNTESS,
THE COUNT, ANTONIO

ANTONIO: (*half tipsy, holding a pot of partly crushed stocks*) My lord! my lord!

COUNT: What do you want of me, Antonio?

ANTONIO: Please have the windows over my beds barred. They throw all sorts of things out of those windows, and even a little while ago they threw out a man.

COUNT: Out of these windows?

ANTONIO: Just look at my stocks!

SUZANNE: (*in a low voice to* FIGARO) Look out, Figaro, look out!

FIGARO: My lord, he is tipsy every day from the crack of dawn.

ANTONIO: You're wrong. It's a little left over from yesterday. That's how one judges you . . . in the dark.

COUNT: (*fiery*) That man, that man, where is he?

ANTONIO: Where he is?

COUNT: Yes.

ANTONIO: That's what I say. I must find him. I'm your servant, I'm the only one to take care of your garden, a man falls on it, and you appreciate . . . that my reputation is tarnished.

SUZANNE: (*in a low voice to* FIGARO) Change the subject, change the subject.

FIGARO: So you'll always drink?

ANTONIO: Why if I didn't drink I'd go mad.

COUNTESS: But to drink so, without thirst . . .

ANTONIO: To drink without thirst and to make love at any time, madam, that's what distinguishes us from the other animals.

COUNT: (*sharply*) Answer me or I'll have you thrown out.

ANTONIO: Would I go?

COUNT: What's that?

ANTONIO: (*touching his forehead*) If you haven't enough of that to keep a good servant, I'm not stupid enough to get rid of so good a master.

COUNT: (*shakes him angrily*) You say they threw a man out of this window?

ANTONIO: Yes, Excellency, just a little while ago, in a white jacket, and who picked himself up and fled . . .

COUNT: (*impatient*) And then?

ANTONIO: I wanted to run after him, but I bumped into the fence so hard my finger is still numb. I can't move either hand or foot of that finger. (*Raising the finger.*)

COUNT: At least you would recognize the man?

ANTONIO: Yes, that I could if I had seen him, however!

SUZANNE: (*in a low voice to* FIGARO) He didn't see him.

FIGARO: What a fuss about a pot of flowers! How long must you carry on with your stocks, whimperer? It's no use seeking, my lord: it was I who jumped down.

COUNT: So it was you?

ANTONIO: "How long must you carry on, whimperer?" Your body must have grown since then? for you were much smaller and thinner at that time!

FIGARO: Certainly; when one jumps, one coils oneself up . . .

ANTONIO: Methought it was rather the whippersnapper of a page I saw.

COUNT: Chérubin, you mean?

FIGARO: Yes, having come back expressly with his horse from the gates of Seville, where perhaps he is already.

ANTONIO: Oh no! I didn't say that, I didn't say that! I didn't see any horse jump, or I'd say so.

COUNT: What patience!

FIGARO: I was in the women's quarters in my white jacket, it was terribly hot! . . . I was waiting there for my Suzannette, when all of a sudden I heard my lord's voice and the great noise that was going on; I don't know what fear seized me about that note . . . And if I must admit my foolishness, I lost my head and jumped down on the flower-beds, where I even sprained my right ankle a little. (*He rubs his foot.*)

ANTONIO: Since it's you, it is right to give you back this bit of paper which fell out of your jacket as you landed.

COUNT: (*snatches it*) Give it to me. (*He unfolds the paper and folds it again.*)

FIGARO: (*aside*) I am caught.

COUNT: (*to* FIGARO) Your fright cannot have made you forget what the paper contains nor how it got into your pocket?

FIGARO: (*embarrassed, rummages in his pockets and brings out some papers*) Surely not . . . But it's because I have so many; everyone must be answered . . . (*He looks at one of the papers.*) This, for example, is a letter of Marceline's, four pages, a beautiful letter . . . Couldn't that other one be the petition from that poor poacher who is in prison? . . . No, here it is . . . I also had a list of the furniture in the little castle in my other pocket . . . (*The* COUNT *reopens the paper in his hand.*)

COUNTESS: (*in a low voice to* SUZANNE) Heavens! Suzy, it's the officer's commission.

SUZANNE: (*in a low voice to* FIGARO) All is lost, it's the commission.

COUNT: (*folds the paper*) Well! resourceful fellow, you can't guess?

ANTONIO: (*approaching* FIGARO)[14] My lord says that you can't guess.

FIGARO: (*pushes him away*) For shame, villein who speaks into my nose.

COUNT: You cannot recall what it might be.

FIGARO: Ah, ah, ah, ah! *povero!* [15] I have it! It must be that wretched child's commission, which he had handed to me and which I forgot to give back. Oh, oh, oh, oh! scatterbrain that I am! What will he do without his commission? We must run after him . . .

COUNT: Why should he have handed it to you?

FIGARO: (*embarrassed*) He . . . wished that something were done to it.

COUNT: (*looks at his paper*) There's nothing missing.

COUNTESS: (*in a low voice to* SUZANNE) The seal.

SUZANNE: (*in a low voice to* FIGARO) The seal's missing.

COUNT: (*to* FIGARO) You are not replying?

---

[14] *Beaumarchais's note: Antonio, Figaro, Suzanne, the Countess, the Count.*

[15] Povero, *the Italian for "poor," "unfortunate," refers to Chérubin.*

FIGARO: The fact is . . . little is missing. He says that it is the custom . . .

COUNT: The custom, the custom! What's the custom?

FIGARO: To affix the seal showing your coat of arms. Maybe it wasn't worth the trouble . . .

COUNT: (*reopens the paper and crumples it angrily*) Confound it! My fate decrees that I shall know nothing. (*aside*) It's Figaro who is the master mind, and I shall not avenge myself? (*He wants to go out because of his spite.*)

FIGARO: (*stopping him*) You're not going without giving the word about my marriage?

SCENE 22

BAZILE, BARTHOLO, MARCELINE, FIGARO, THE COUNT, GRIPPE-SOLEIL, THE COUNTESS, SUZANNE, ANTONIO, THE COUNT'S VALETS, HIS VASSALS

MARCELINE: (*to the* COUNT) Do not give the word, my lord; before you do him a favor, you owe us justice. He has obligations toward me.

COUNT: (*aside*) My revenge has come at last!

FIGARO: Obligations? Of what kind? Explain.

MARCELINE: Yes, I shall explain, scoundrel! . . . (*The* COUNTESS *sits in an easy chair,* SUZANNE *is behind her.*)

COUNT: What is it all about, Marceline?

MARCELINE: A promise of marriage.

FIGARO: A promissory note for money she lent me, that's all.

MARCELINE: (*to the* COUNT) But on condition of marrying me. You are a great lord, the first judge of the province . . .

COUNT: Come to the assizes; I will give everybody justice there.

BAZILE: (*pointing to* MARCELINE) In that case, Your Worship will permit me also to assert my claims on Marceline.

COUNT: (*aside*) That is the scoundrel of the note.

FIGARO: Another madman of the same kind!

COUNT: (*to* BAZILE, *angrily*) Your claims! Your claims! What right have you to speak up in my presence, master fool?

ANTONIO: (*striking his fist in his other hand*) Indeed, he didn't miss it the first time; it is his right name.

COUNT: Marceline, everything will be suspended until the public hearing of your claims, which shall take place in the large reception hall. Wise Bazile, my faithful and reliable agent, go into town to summon the bench.

BAZILE: For her case?

COUNT: And you shall bring along the peasant who gave you the note.

BAZILE: Do I know him?

COUNT: You object!

BAZILE: I did not enter the castle to run errands.

COUNT: What, then?

BAZILE: A talented performer on the parish organ, I teach madam the harpsichord, her women to sing, and your pages the mandolin. But my main employment is to entertain your company on my guitar, when it pleases you to command me.

GRIPPE-SOLEIL: (*comes forward*) I'll go, my lord, if that's what you want.

COUNT: What's your name and your employment?

GRIPPE-SOLEIL: My name is Grippe-Soleil, my good lord. I am the little goatherd, asked in for the fireworks. It's a holiday today for us in the herds, and I know where's the rabid trial-shop in town.

COUNT: Your zeal pleases me, go do my errand. But as for you (*to* BAZILE) accompany the gentleman, singing and playing the guitar to entertain him on the way. He is of my company.

GRIPPE-SOLEIL: (*elated*) Oh! I, I'm of the . . . (SUZANNE *soothes him with her hand pointing to the* COUNTESS.)

BAZILE: (*surprised*) I must accompany Grippe-Soleil while playing?

COUNT: It is your profession; off you go, or I'll dismiss you. (*Exit.*)

SCENE 23

THE PRECEDING ACTORS, *except the Count*

BAZILE: (*to himself*) Oh! I'm not going to fight the iron pot, I who am only . . .

FIGARO: A jug.[16]

BAZILE: (*aside*) Instead of furthering their marriage, I'm going to insure Marceline's and mine. (*To* FIGARO) Don't conclude anything, believe me, until I come back. (*He goes to pick up his guitar from the chair in the rear.*)

FIGARO: (*follows him*) Conclude anything? Oh! Don't worry, fear nothing, even if you never come back . . . But you don't look like one who wants to sing; would you like me to begin? Come on, be gay, and the high la-mi-la for my fiancée. (*He walks backwards and dances the following seguedilla;* BAZILE *accompanies him and everybody joins in.*)

SEGUEDILLA: (*A well-known tune*)
Better than riches, I like
The goodness of
My Suzy;
Zy, zy, zy,

---

[16] *Two proverbs are involved here:* 1) C'est le pot de terre contre le pot de fer (*cf. La Fontaine's fable*); 2) Tant va la cruche à l'eau, qu'à la fin elle se casse. *The first is said when one is up against more than one's match; the second means "So often does the jug go to the well that it is broken at last."*

Zy, zy, zy,
Zy, zy, zy,
Zy, zy, zy.

Her graciousness, too,
Is mistress of
My reason;
Son, son, son,
Son, son, son,
Son, son, son,
Son, son, son.

(*The noise dies down, the remainder is not heard.*)

SCENE 24

SUZANNE, THE COUNTESS

COUNTESS: (*in her easy chair*) You see, Suzanne, the row I had to put up with, thanks to your harebrained friend with his note.

SUZANNE: Oh, madam, if you had only seen your face, when I came out of the dressing-room! You lost your color all of a sudden, but only for a moment and gradually you grew red, red, oh so red!

COUNTESS: So he jumped out of the window?

SUZANNE: Without hesitation, the darling child! Light . . . as a bird!

COUNTESS: That terrible gardener! The whole thing moved me to the extent . . . that I couldn't put two ideas together in my mind.

SUZANNE: Oh, madam, on the contrary; and that's when I saw what facility the habit of high society bestows upon respectable ladies as to how to lie without seeming to.

COUNTESS: Do you believe the Count was taken in by it? and suppose he found the child in the castle?

SUZANNE: I am going to advise that he be well hidden . . .

COUNTESS: He must leave. After what has just happened, you can well imagine I'm not tempted to send him in the garden in your place.

SUZANNE: It's certain I shan't go either. So once again my marriage is . . .

COUNTESS: (*rises*) Wait. Instead of another or you, suppose I went there myself?

SUZANNE: You, madam?

COUNTESS: No one would be exposed . . . besides the Count could not deny . . . To have punished his jealousy and to prove his infidelity! that would be . . . Come, our luck in our first adventure emboldens me to attempt the second. Let him know quickly that you will go into the garden. But be sure nobody . . .

SUZANNE: Not even Figaro?

COUNTESS: No, no. He would like to contribute his own ideas . . . My velvet mask and my stick, so I can go out on the terrace and daydream. (*Suzanne goes into the dressing-room.*)

SCENE 25

THE COUNTESS: (*alone*) My little scheme is brazen enough! (*She turns around*) Ah! my ribbon, my pretty ribbon, I had forgotten you! (*She takes it from the easy chair and rolls it up*) Henceforth you will never leave me . . . you will remind me of the scene in which that unfortunate boy . . . Oh, Count, what have you done? And what am I doing right now?

SCENE 26

THE COUNTESS, SUZANNE

(*The* COUNTESS *furtively slips the ribbon into her bosom.*)

SUZANNE: Here is the stick and your mask.

COUNTESS: Remember that I have forbidden you to say one word to Figaro.

SUZANNE: (*joyful*) Your plan, madam, is charming. I've just been thinking about it. It brings everything together, concludes everything, embraces everything, and whatever may happen, my marriage is now certain. (*She kisses her mistress's hand.*) (*Exeunt.*)

During the intermission, servants prepare the courtroom: two benches with backs are brought in for the attorneys, on each side of the stage, but allowing free passage behind. In the center, toward the rear, a platform with two steps, on which is placed the Count's chair. The clerk's table and his stool are put to one side downstage, and chairs for Brid'oison and the other judges are placed on both sides of the Count's platform.

ACT THREE

The stage represents a room in the castle called the throne room and used as a reception hall, having on one side a monumental canopy, and underneath, the King's portrait.

SCENE 1

THE COUNT, PÉDRILLE, *who is wearing jacket and boots and is holding a sealed package*

COUNT: (*fast*) Have you understood me clearly?

PÉDRILLE: Yes, Your Excellency. (*Exit.*)

SCENE 2

COUNT: (*alone, shouting*) Pédrille!

SCENE 3

THE COUNT, PÉDRILLE *comes back*

PÉDRILLE: Excellency?

COUNT: No one saw you?

PÉDRILLE: Not a soul.

COUNT: Take the Barbary horse.

PÉDRILLE: He's at the garden gate, all saddled.

COUNT: Straight to Seville without a stop.

PÉDRILLE: It's only three leagues but the road is not so good.

COUNT: When you arrive, find out if the page is there.

PÉDRILLE: In the hotel?

COUNT: Yes, and above all how long he's been there.

PÉDRILLE: I understand.

COUNT: Give him his commission and come back quickly.

PÉDRILLE: And suppose he should not be there?

COUNT: Come back even more quickly and tell me about it. Be off!

SCENE 4

COUNT: (*alone, paces as he meditates*) It was awkward of me to get rid of Bazile! . . . Anger is good for nothing. The note he handed me warning me of an attempt to see the Countess . . . The chambermaid locked up when I arrive . . . Her mistress making believe she was terrified, or actually terrified . . . A man jumping out of the window and the other, later, admitting it or contending that it was he. There is something missing. There is something devious in it. Some license among my vassals, what does it matter to people of that sort? But the Countess! If some impudent fellow should attempt . . . Where does my mind wander? Truly, when anger has the upper hand, the most controlled imagination runs wild, as in a dream. She was having a good time; that smothered laughter, that ill-concealed joy! She has self-respect, and my honor . . . in whose keeping is it? On the other hand, where do I stand? Did that roguish Suzanne betray my secret? As it isn't hers! . . . What chains me to this whim? I wanted to give it up twenty times . . . Strange results of indecision! If I wanted her without hesitation, I should desire her a thousand times less. That Figaro certainly keeps me waiting! I must cleverly plumb his thoughts (FIGARO *appears in the rear; he stops*), and try to find out in a casual manner in the conversation I'm going to have with him whether or not he knows I'm in love with Suzanne.

SCENE 5

THE COUNT, FIGARO

FIGARO: (*aside*) Here we are.

COUNT: . . . if she has dropped a single word to him . . .

FIGARO: (*aside*) I suspected as much.

COUNT: . . . I marry him off to the old girl.

FIGARO: (*aside*) Mr. Bazile's beloved?

COUNT: . . . And let's see what we can do with the young one.

FIGARO: (*aside*) With my wife, if you please.

COUNT: (*turns around*) Hey! what? what is it?

FIGARO: (*comes forward*) Me, at your service.

COUNT: And why these words?

FIGARO: I haven't said anything.

COUNT: (*repeats*) "My wife, if you please?"

FIGARO: It's . . . the end of a reply: "Go and say it to my wife, if you please."

COUNT: (*paces*) "His wife!" . . . I should like to know what business can detain your lordship when I have you called?

FIGARO: (*making believe he is adjusting his clothing*) I had got dirty falling on those beds, so I changed.

COUNT: Does it take an hour?

FIGARO: It takes time.

COUNT: The servants here . . . need longer to dress than the masters!

FIGARO: That's because they have no valets to help them.

COUNT: . . . I did not quite understand what forced you a little while ago to risk your life uselessly by jumping . . .

FIGARO: Risk my life! One would think that I had leaped into a bottomless pit . . .

COUNT: Try to put me off the track by pretending you were deceived, you devious valet! You understand very well that it isn't the danger that concerns me, but your motive.

FIGARO: Owing to a false alarm, you come rushing in furiously, upsetting everything like the torrent of the

Morena;[1] you're looking for a man, you have to find him or you are going to break down the doors, burst in the walls! I happen to be here: who knows whether in your wrath . . .

COUNT: (*interrupting*) You could have fled by the stairs.

FIGARO: And you catch me in the hall.

COUNT: (*angry*) In the hall? (*aside*) I am in a temper and I cannot find out what I am after.

FIGARO: (*aside*) Let's see what he's driving at and play a cautious game.

COUNT: (*his tone softened*) That isn't what I meant. Let's drop the subject. I was thinking . . . yes, I did think of taking you with me to London, as King's Messenger; . . . but, on second thought . . .

FIGARO: My lord has changed his mind?

COUNT: In the first place you don't know English.

FIGARO: I know "God-dam."

COUNT: Well?

FIGARO: The dickens! English is a beautiful language; it takes only little to go a long way. With "God-dam," in England, one need lack for nothing nowhere. Do you want to sink your teeth into a nice fat fowl? Go into a tavern and make only this gesture to the waiter (*he turns a spit*), saying "God-dam!", he brings you a joint of salt beef without bread. It's marvelous! Do you like a good glass of burgundy or claret? Just do this (*he draws a cork*). "God-dam!", they bring you a foaming tankard of beer. It's

[1] *The Sierra Morena is a mountain range in Southwest Spain.*

wonderful! Should you meet one of those pretty ladies who go trotting about with their eyes lowered, their elbows pulled back, and their hips swinging a little, just put all your fingers affectedly on your lips. "God-dam!", she gives you a slap like a porter. That proves she understands. The English truly add some other words, here and there in their conversation; but it is quite easy to see that "God-dam" is the core of the language; so if my lord has no other reason for leaving me behind in Spain . . .

COUNT: (*aside*) He wants to go to London; she has not talked.

FIGARO: (*aside*) He believes I know nothing; let's encourage him a little in his delusion.

COUNT: What motive had the Countess for playing that trick on me?

FIGARO: Indeed, my lord, you know it better than I.

COUNT: I anticipate all her wishes and lavish her with gifts.

FIGARO: You give but you are unfaithful. Is one grateful for luxuries to him who deprives us of necessities?

COUNT: . . . Some time ago you used to tell me everything.

FIGARO: And now I hide nothing from you.

COUNT: How much did the Countess give you for being in league with her?

FIGARO: How much did you give me to wrest her from the doctor's hands? [2] Look here, my lord, do not humiliate

---

[2] *Figaro helped Count Almaviva to wrest Rosine from Bartholo.* See The Barber of Seville.

the man who serves one well, for fear he may turn into a nasty valet.

COUNT: Why must there always be something suspicious in what you do?

FIGARO: One sees suspicion everywhere when one is bent on finding fault.

COUNT: You have a hateful reputation!

FIGARO: What if I'm worth more than my reputation? Are there many noblemen who can say as much?

COUNT: A hundred times I've seen you on the path to fame and fortune, and you never went straight.

FIGARO: What do you expect? The mob is all around; each one wants to run; there is hustling, pushing, elbowing, overturning; succeed who can, the rest are crushed. And so my mind's made up; I give up.

COUNT: Give up success? (*aside*) That's new.

FIGARO: (*aside*) My turn now. (*aloud*) Your Excellency has bestowed upon me the stewardship of the castle; it's a very happy lot. Of course, I shan't be King's Messenger, the first to hear interesting news, but to compensate for it, I'll live in wedded bliss in the heart of Andalusia . . .

COUNT: Who would prevent you from taking your wife to London?

FIGARO: I'd have to leave her so often that I'd soon find marriage a bore.

COUNT: With your character and your brains, you could make your way in the administration.

FIGARO: Make my way with brains? My lord makes fun of mine. Be mediocre and obsequious and you'll succeed in everything.

COUNT: . . . All you'd have to do is to study some state-craft under me.

FIGARO: I know it.

COUNT: As you do English: the core of the language!

FIGARO: Yes, if there were something to boast about; but to pretend not to know what you do know, to know all that you do not know, to understand what you do not understand, not to hear what you do hear, above all to do what is beyond your strength; to make often a great secret of what no one is hiding; to lock yourself up and trim quills so as to appear profound when you are only, as they say, hollow inside; to play a part well or badly, send out spies and retire traitors, tamper with seals, intercept letters, and attempt to make ignoble means look noble in the light of important ends: that's all of statecraft or Heaven strike me dead!

COUNT: But that's intrigue you're describing!

FIGARO: Statecraft, intrigue, whatever you wish; but as I believe to be a bit kindred, everybody is welcome to them! "I'd rather have my own best girl!" [3] as the good king's ballad says.

COUNT: (aside) He wants to remain. I see . . . Suzanne has betrayed me.

[3] J'aime mieux ma mie, o gué, *a song of the time of Henry IV, is quoted in Molière's* Misanthrope.

FIGARO: (*aside*) I've won and paid him back in kind.

COUNT: And so you hope to win your case against Marceline?

FIGARO: Would you consider it a crime to refuse an old maid when Your Excellency feels free to snatch all the young ones?

COUNT: (*bantering*) On the bench the judge forgets himself and will heed nothing but the law.

FIGARO: Lenient to the great, harsh to the humble . . .

COUNT: Do you think I am jesting?

FIGARO: Well! Who knows, my lord? *Tempo è galant'uomo,*[4] says the Italian; it always tells the truth: it will tell me who wishes me harm or good.

COUNT: (*aside*) I can see she has told him everything; he shall marry the duenna.

FIGARO: (*aside*) He thinks he has me fooled; really, what has he learned?

SCENE 6

THE COUNT, A LACKEY, FIGARO

LACKEY: (*announcing*) Don Guzman Brid'oison.

COUNT: Brid'oison?

FIGARO: Well, naturally. He's the associate justice, the lieutenant of the bench, your right-hand man.

COUNT: Let him wait. (*Exit* LACKEY.)

---

[4] *The Italian means "Time is a man of integrity and honor." Today one would say* Il tempo è galantuomo.

SCENE 7

THE COUNT, FIGARO

FIGARO: (*waits a moment longer while the* COUNT *muses*) Is that what my lord wanted?

COUNT: (*becoming himself again*) I? . . . I was saying this hall should be prepared for the public hearing.

FIGARO: Well! what does it lack? the large chair for you, good chairs for the justices, the clerk's stool, two benches for the attorneys, the foreground for high society and the groundlings behind. I'm going to send away the cleaners.
(*Exit.*)

SCENE 8

COUNT: (*alone*) That rascal is becoming a nuisance! When he argues he gets the best of you, he presses in and corners you . . . Ah! fox and vixen! you have combined to trick me. Be friends, be lovers, be what you like, I don't care. But, indeed, when it comes to marrying . . .

SCENE 9

SUZANNE, THE COUNT

SUZANNE: (*out of breath*) My lord, . . . forgive me, my lord.

COUNT: (*crossly*) What is the matter, miss?

SUZANNE: You are angry?

COUNT: You want something apparently?

SUZANNE: It's because my mistress has her vapors. I ran to beg you to lend us your bottle of smelling salts. I'll bring it back right away.

COUNT: (*gives it to her*) No, no, keep it for yourself, you'll soon need it.

SUZANNE: Do women of my kind have vapors, too? It's a class disease, which is caught only in boudoirs.

COUNT: A fiancée who is very much in love and who loses her intended.

SUZANNE: What if he pays Marceline out of the dowry you promised me.

COUNT: I promised you?

SUZANNE: (*lowering her eyes*) My lord, I believe I heard you say so.

COUNT: Yes, but only if you were willing to listen to me yourself.

SUZANNE: (*her eyes lowered*) And isn't it my duty to listen to His Excellency?

COUNT: Then why, cruel girl, didn't you tell me sooner?

SUZANNE: Is it ever too late to tell the truth?

COUNT: You are going to the garden at dusk.

SUZANNE: Don't I walk there every evening?

COUNT: This morning you behaved so harshly to me!

SUZANNE: This morning? . . . How about the page behind the armchair?

COUNT: She is right, I forgot. But why that stubborn refusal, when Bazile, on my behalf? . . .

SUZANNE: Why should someone like Bazile? . . .

COUNT: She is always right. Nevertheless, there is a certain Figaro to whom I fear you have told everything.

SUZANNE: Why, of course I tell him everything, except what need be kept quiet.

COUNT: (laughing) You darling! So you promise me? If you should break your word, let's be clear about it, sweetheart: no rendezvous, no dowry, no marriage.

SUZANNE: (curtsying) But by the same token, my lord, no marriage, no right of the lord of the manor.

COUNT: Where does she learn what she says? I swear, I'll go mad. But your mistress is waiting for the bottle . . .

SUZANNE: (laughing and giving back the bottle) Could I have talked to you without a pretext?

COUNT: (wants to kiss her) Delightful creature!

SUZANNE: People are coming.

COUNT: (aside) She is mine. (He runs off.)

SUZANNE: (runs off) I must go quickly to report to madam.

SCENE 10

SUZANNE, FIGARO

FIGARO: Suzanne, Suzanne! Where are you running so quickly after leaving my lord?

SUZANNE: Go to court now if you want; you've just won your case. (*She runs off.*)

FIGARO: (*follows her*) But see here . . .

SCENE 11

COUNT: (*returns alone*) "You've just won your case!" So I was getting into a nice trap! O my dear impertinent schemers, I'll punish you in such a way . . . A good, a very just decision . . . But suppose he were to pay off the duenna . . . With what? Suppose he should pay . . . Ah, ah, haven't I the proud Antonio, whose noble pride scorns in Figaro one who is without roots and unworthy of his niece? By nursing this fixation . . . And why not? In the vast field of intrigue, one must cultivate everything, even the vanity of fools. (*He calls*) Anto . . . (*He sees* MARCELINE *and others*) (*Exit.*)

SCENE 12

BARTHOLO, MARCELINE, BRID'OISON

MARCELINE: (*to* BRID'OISON) Sir, please listen to my case.

BRID'OISON: (*gowned and stuttering slightly*) Very well, let us ta-talk about it.

BARTHOLO: It's a promise of marriage.

MARCELINE: Linked with a loan of money.

BRID'OISON: I und-understand, *etcetera,* the rest.

MARCELINE: No, sir, no *etcetera.*

BRID'OISON: I und-understand; do you have the money?

MARCELINE: No, sir, it was I who lent it.

BRID'OISON: I quite und-understand; you-you want the money back?

MARCELINE: No, sir; I require him to marry me.

BRID'OISON: But I und-understand quite well; and he, does he wa-want to marry you?

MARCELINE: No, sir; that's the whole point of the suit!

BRID'OISON: Do you think that I do not und-understand the suit?

MARCELINE: No, sir. (*To* BARTHOLO) What a predicament we're in! (*To* BRID'OISON) What! are you going to decide the case?

BRID'OISON: Why else would I have bought my ju-judgeship?

MARCELINE: (*sighing*). It's a great wrong to sell them!

BRID'OISON: True, one-one would do better to give them to us for nothing: Whom are you su-suing?

SCENE 13

BARTHOLO, MARCELINE, BRID'OISON; FIGARO, *enters rubbing his hands*

MARCELINE: (*pointing to* FIGARO) Sir, that unscrupulous man.

FIGARO: (*very cheerfully to* MARCELINE) Perhaps I bother you.—My lord will be back in a moment, Your Worship.

BRID'OISON: I've seen that f-fellow somewhere.

FIGARO: In the house of your wife, at Seville, in her service, counselor.

BRID'OISON: In wha-what year?

FIGARO: A little less than a year before the birth of your younger son, who is a very pretty child if I do say so myself.

BRID'OISON: Yes, he is the pre-prettiest of them all. They tell me here that you-you are up to your old tricks?

FIGARO: You flatter me, sir. It's only a trifle.

BRID'OISON: A promise of marriage. What a booby he is!

FIGARO: Sir . . .

BRID'OISON: Has he seen my-my secretary, that nice fellow?

FIGARO: You mean Double-Main, the clerk?

BRID'OISON: Yes, I do. He fee-feeds in two places.

FIGARO: Feeds! I'll swear he devours. Oh! yes indeed, I saw him about the writ, and about the supplement to the writ, as is customary, anyway.

BRID'OISON: Forms must be ob-observed.

FIGARO: Of course, sir: if the cause of suits belongs to the litigants, we know very well that forms are the property of courts.

BRID'OISON: That lad is-is not so stupid as I thought at first. Very well, friend, since you know so much, we'll ta-take care of your case.

FIGARO: Sir, I rely on your sense of equity although you are one of our justices.

BRID'OISON: What? . . . Yes, I am a justice. But suppose you owe and do-do not pay? . . .

FIGARO: Then you can surely see it's as if I didn't owe.

BRID'OISON: No d-doubt. What? What did he say?

SCENE 14

BARTHOLO, MARCELINE, THE COUNT, BRID'OISON,
FIGARO, AN USHER

USHER: (*walking ahead of the* COUNT, *exclaims*) My lord, gentlemen!

COUNT: Gowns in this place, Master Brid'oison! it's only a domestic hearing. Ordinary clothes are good enough.

BRID'OISON: It's you who are good, my lord. But I never go ung-ungowned, don't you see, it is a matter of form, of form. One will laugh at a judge in a short coat but tr-tremble at the mere sight of an attorney in a gown, thanks to the form, the f-form.

COUNT: (*to the* USHER) Let the court convene.

USHER: (*goes to open the door as he yaps*) The court!

SCENE 15

THE PRECEDING ACTORS, ANTONIO, THE SERVANTS OF THE CASTLE, PEASANT MEN AND WOMEN, *in holiday clothes; the* COUNT *sits in a big chair;* BRID'OISON, *on a chair to one side; the* CLERK, *on a stool behind his table; the* JUDGES, *the* LAWYERS, *on the benches;* MARCELINE, *beside* BARTHOLO; FIGARO, *on the other bench; the* PEASANTS *and* SERVANTS *standing behind them*

BRID'OISON: (*to* DOUBLE-MAIN) Double-Main, c-call up the cases.

DOUBLE-MAIN: (*reads from a paper*) The noble, very noble, infinitely noble Don Pedro George, Hidalgo and Baron de los Altos y Montes Fieros y otros montes versus Alonzo Calderón, a young playwright. It is the matter of a still-born play, which each disowns and lays on the other.

COUNT: They are both right. Case dismissed. If they do

another work together, in order to insure public attention, it is ordered that the nobleman shall contribute his name and the poet his talent.

DOUBLE-MAIN: (*reads from another paper*) André Pétrutchio, farmer, versus the tax collector of the province. It is the matter of an arbitrary foreclosure.

COUNT: The case is not within my jurisdiction. I shall serve my vassals best by patronizing them at the King's court. Next.

DOUBLE-MAIN: (*takes a third paper.* BARTHOLO *and* FIGARO *rise.*) Barbe-Agar-Raab-Magdelaine-Nicole-Marceline de Verte-Allure, a maid of age (MARCELINE *rises and bows*) versus Figaro . . . first name not given?

FIGARO: Anonymous.

BRID'OISON: An-anonymous? What patron s-saint is that?

FIGARO: It's mine.

DOUBLE-MAIN (*writes*) Versus Anonymous Figaro. Profession?

FIGARO: Gentleman.

COUNT: You're a gentleman? (*The* CLERK *is writing.*)

FIGARO: If Heaven had so wished, I should have been a prince's son.

COUNT: (*to the* CLERK) Go on.

USHER: (*yapping*) Silence in the court!

DOUBLE-MAIN: (*reads*) . . . In the matter of the opposition made to the marriage of the said Figaro by the said Verte-Allure. Doctor Bartholo appearing for the plaintiff and the said Figaro for himself, if the court allows it against the wishes of custom and the rules of the bench.

FIGARO: Custom, Master Double-Main, is often an abuse. A party to a suit, who is but a little educated, always knows his case better than some attorney, who, sweating without conviction, shouting his head off, and knowing everything, except the facts, does not trouble himself to ruin the suitor nor does he mind boring the court and putting the jury to sleep. Afterwards, he is more puffed up than if he had composed the *Oratio pro Murena*.[5] I shall put my case in few words. Gentlemen . . .

DOUBLE-MAIN: Those you've said so far are useless, for you are not the plaintiff and you can only defend. Come forward, doctor, and read the promise.

FIGARO: Yes, the promise!

BARTHOLO: (*putting on his glasses*) It is explicit.

BRID'OISON: We-we have to see.

DOUBLE-MAIN: Gentlemen, silence please!

USHER: (*yapping*) Silence in the court!

BARTHOLO: (*reads*) "I, the undersigned, acknowledge having received from the damsel, etc. . . . Marceline de Verte-Allure, in the manor of Aguas-Frescas, the sum of two thousand edge-rolled piastres,[6] which sum I shall repay on her demand in said manor, and I shall marry her as a token of gratitude, etc. signed Figaro, just Figaro." My opinion is that the note should be paid and that the promise should

---

[5] *One of Cicero's orations. The* Oratio pro Murena *is aptly mentioned because jurisconsults are satirized, among others.*

[6] *Usually a coin of silver, the "piastre" has various values.*

be executed, with costs. (*He pleads.*) Gentlemen . . . never was a more interesting case brought to the Bar of Justice! and since Alexander the Great, who promised marriage to the beautiful Thalestris[7] . . .

COUNT: (*interrupting*) Before going further, counsel, is the genuineness of the document agreed upon?

BRID'OISON: (*to* FIGARO) What do you say to the f-facts just read?

FIGARO: I say, gentlemen, there is malice, error or in-advertence in the manner in which the document was read; for the statement does not say: "which sum I shall repay *and* I shall marry her," but: "which sum I shall repay *or* I shall marry her," which is quite different.

COUNT: Does the document say *and* or else *or*?

BARTHOLO: It says *and*.

FIGARO: It says *or*.

BRID'OISON: Dou-ouble-Main, you read it.

DOUBLE-MAIN: (*taking the paper*) That's surer, because the parties often twist things as they read. Er-er-er- "Dam-sel" -er-er-er- "de Verte-Allure" -er-er-er. Ha! "Which sum I shall repay on her demand, in the said manor" . . . *And* . . . *or* . . . *and* . . . *or* . . . The word is so badly written . . . there is a blot.

BRID'OISON: A b-blot? I know what it is.

BARTHOLO: (*pleading*) I submit that it is the copulative conjunction *and* which links the correlative members of the sentence: "I shall pay the damsel *and* I shall marry her."

[7] *Thalestris, queen of the Amazons, bore Alexander the Great a child.*

FIGARO: (*pleading*) And I contend that it is the alternating conjunction *or,* which separates the said members: "I shall pay the damsel *or* I shall marry her." To his pedantry I oppose my superpedantry; if he takes it into his head to speak Latin, I shall speak Greek. I'll exterminate him.

COUNT: How can we adjudicate such a question?

BARTHOLO: To settle it, gentlemen, and no longer quibble over a word, we admit that there is an *or.*

FIGARO: I ask for an affidavit to that effect.

BARTHOLO: And we stand by our admission. But it affords no escape for the guilty one; let us examine the document with the change in mind. (*He reads.*) "Which sum I shall repay in this manor where[8] I shall marry her"; it's as if one would say, gentlemen; "you will have yourself bled in this bed where you will remain snugly"; where means in which. "He will take a dose of rhubarb where you will mix a little tamarind"; in which you will mix. Thus "the manor where I shall marry her," gentlemen, "is the manor in which . . ."

FIGARO: Not at all; the sentence has the meaning of this one: "Either illness will carry you off *or* your physician will," or else "your physician" without the "will," it's irrefutable whichever way. Another example: "Either you will write nothing pleasing *or* fools will disparage you"; or else "fools" without "will disparage you," the sense is clear either way: for, in said case, "fools" or "the wicked" is the

[8] *French "or" and "where" are written respectively* ou *and* où; *moreover,* où *may be used for* dans lequel, *"in which." Many Frenchmen do not write accents.*

governing noun. Does Dr. Bartholo think I have forgotten my grammar? Thus, I shall pay her in this manor, *comma*, *or* I shall marry her . . .

BARTHOLO: (*quickly*) No comma.

FIGARO: (*quickly*) There is. It goes "comma," gentlemen, "or else I shall marry her."

BARTHOLO: (*looking at the paper, quickly*) Without a comma, gentlemen.

FIGARO: (*quickly*) It was there, gentlemen. Moreover, is a man who marries obliged to pay the debt?

BARTHOLO: (*quickly*) Yes, we marry under a separate property agreement.

FIGARO: (*quickly*) If marriage does not cancel the debt, we insist on the separation of persons and property. (*The* JUDGES *rise and confer in a very low voice.*)

BARTHOLO: A fine cancellation.

DOUBLE-MAIN: Silence, gentlemen!

USHER: (*yapping*) Silence in the court!

BARTHOLO: Such a scoundrel calls that paying his debts!

FIGARO: Are you pleading your own case, counsel?

BARTHOLO: I am defending this lady.

FIGARO: Go on raving, but stop insulting. When the law, fearing the temper of the litigants, permitted the intervention of counsel, it did not mean that these temperate defenders should become with impunity privileged insolent fellows. That would have been to degrade the noblest of institutions.

(*The* JUDGES *are still conferring in a low voice.*)

ANTONIO: (*to* MARCELINE *and pointing to the* JUDGES) What do they have to say?

MARCELINE: They have corrupted the chief justice; he is corrupting the other one; and I am about to lose my case.

BARTHOLO: (*in a low voice, somberly*) I am afraid so.

FIGARO: (*gayly*) Cheer up, Marceline!

DOUBLE-MAIN (*rises; to* MARCELINE) Ah! that's too much! I denounce you, and for the honor of the Court I ask that before the other case is settled, it settle this one.

COUNT: (*sits down*) No, clerk, I shall not judge for an insult to my person. No Spanish judge will have to blush for an abuse of power, worthy at most of oriental courts. We commit enough wrongs as it is. I am now going to correct one of these by giving the reasons for my decision: any judge who refuses to do so is a great enemy of the law! What can the plaintiff ask? Marriage failing payment; both together would imply a contradiction.

DOUBLE-MAIN: Silence, gentlemen!

USHER: (*yapping*) Silence in the court!

COUNT: What does the defendant reply? that he wants to retain possession of his person. Permission is granted.

FIGARO: (*with joy*) I've won.

COUNT: But as the text says: "Which sum I shall pay on the first demand *or* else I shall marry, etc.," the Count condemns the defendant to pay the plaintiff two thousand piastres *or* else to marry her within the day. (*He gets up.*)

FIGARO: (*amazed*) I've lost.

ANTONIO: (*joyful*) Magnificent decision.

FIGARO: How, magnificent?

ANTONIO: On account of how you're no longer my nephew. Many thanks, my lord!

USHER: (*yapping*) Move along, gentlemen. (*Exeunt.*)

ANTONIO: I'm off to tell all about it to my niece. (*Exit.*)

SCENE 16

THE COUNT, *going from side to side;* MARCELINE,
BARTHOLO, FIGARO, BRID'OISON

MARCELINE: (*sits down*) Now I can breathe freely.

FIGARO: But I am stifling.

COUNT: (*aside*) At least I am avenged; that's soothing.

FIGARO: (*aside*) And that Bazile, who was supposed to prevent Marceline's marriage, see how he's back! (*To the* COUNT *leaving*) You're leaving us already, my lord?

COUNT: Everything is judged.

FIGARO: (*to* BRID'OISON) It's that big, puffed up justice . . .

BRID'OISON: I, big, puffed up!

FIGARO: No doubt about it. And I shan't marry her; I am a gentleman at least once. (*The* COUNT *stops.*)

BARTHOLO: You shall marry her.

FIGARO: Without my noble parents' consent?

BARTHOLO: Name them, exhibit them.

FIGARO: Give me a little time; I am quite close to seeing them again, I've been looking for them for fifteen years.

BARTHOLO: Conceited ass! He must be some foundling!

FIGARO: A lost child, doctor, or rather, stolen.

COUNT: (*returns*) "Stolen, lost?" Where's the proof? Otherwise he'd cry out that they are wronging him!

FIGARO: My lord, even if the lace on my baby clothes, the embroidered coverlet, and the golden jewels found on my person by the brigands, did not prove my high birth, the care that had been taken to put distinctive marks on me would show sufficiently that I was a valuable offspring: and this hieroglyphic on my arm . . . (*He wants to roll up his right sleeve.*)

MARCELINE: (*rising quickly*) A spatula on your right arm?

FIGARO: How do you know I must have it?

MARCELINE: Heavens, it's he.

FIGARO: Of course it's I.

BARTHOLO: (*to* MARCELINE) Who? he!

MARCELINE: (*quickly*) It's Emmanuel.

BARTHOLO: (*to* FIGARO) You were kidnapped by gypsies?

FIGARO: (*excited*) Very near a castle. My good doctor, if you restore me to my noble family, set a high price on your services; heaps of gold are trifles to my illustrious parents.

BARTHOLO: (*pointing to* MARCELINE) There is your mother.

FIGARO: . . . Foster mother?

BARTHOLO: Your own mother.

COUNT: His mother!

FIGARO: Explain.

MARCELINE: (*pointing to* BARTHOLO) There is your father.

FIGARO: (*grieved*) Oh, oh, oh! woe is me!

MARCELINE: Didn't the voice of nature tell you time and again?

FIGARO: Never.

COUNT: (*aside*) His mother!

BRID'OISON: One thing is c-clear: he won't marry her.

BARTHOLO:[9] Nor I either.

MARCELINE: Nor you! And your son? You had sworn to me . . .

BARTHOLO: I was insane. If such pledges held, one would be obliged to marry everybody.

BRID'OISON: And if one were so p-particular about it, nobody would marry anybody.

BARTHOLO: Indiscretions so well-known! a deplorable youth!

MARCELINE: (*getting gradually excited*) Yes, deplorable, and more than you think. I do not mean to deny my indiscretions, today has shown them only too well! But how hard it is to atone for them after thirty years of a modest life! I was born to be good, and so I became as soon as I was allowed to use my reason. But in the period of illusions, inexperience, and needs, when seducers beset us, while poverty assails us, what can a child do against so many enemies gathered together? A man judges us here

---

[9] *Beaumarchais's note: What follows has been deleted by the actors of the Comédie Française in Parisian performances of the play.*

severely, who maybe in his lifetime ruined ten unfortunate girls!

FIGARO: The most guilty are the least generous; that's the rule.

MARCELINE: (*with animation*) Men more than ungrateful, who blight by scorn the playthings of your passions, your victims, it is you who should be punished for the indiscretions of our youth. You and your magistrates, so vain about the right of judging us, and who, by their guilty negligence, allow all honest means of subsistence to be taken from us. Is there a single profession open to women? They have a natural right to every adornment of women. A thousand workers of the other sex are allowed to be trained.

FIGARO: (*angry*) They even make soldiers do embroidery work!

MARCELINE: (*excited*) Even in the highest ranks, women get from you only derisory consideration: lured by apparent respect, but in a real servitude; treated as minors for our own property, punished like those of age for our indiscretions! Ah, in every respect, your behavior toward us arouses our horror or our pity.

FIGARO: She is right!

COUNT: (*aside*) Only too right!

BRID'OISON: B-by God, she is right.

MARCELINE: But what is the refusal of an unjust man to us, my son? Do not look where you came from, see where you're going; that is all that's important to each of us. In a few months your fiancée will no longer depend on anyone but herself; she will accept you, I vouch for it. Live between a tender wife and mother, who will vie with each other in their love for you. Be lenient towards them, happy yourself, my son; gay, free, and good with everybody: your mother will want for nothing.

FIGARO: You speak words of gold, mamma, and I'll abide by your opinion. Indeed, how people are foolish! The world has been rolling for thousands of years, and in this ocean of duration in which by chance I've had some thirty years which will never come back, I should go and torment myself to know to whom I am indebted for them! So much the worse for those who care! To spend life thus squabbling is to weigh down the collar relentlessly like those wretched horses who go upstream, who never rest even when they stop, and who keep on dragging although they stop going. We'll wait.[10]

COUNT: Stupid turn of events. It's annoying.

BRID'OISON. And your nobility, your castle? You are hoodwinking the l-law.

FIGARO: The law! It was going to make me commit a fine blunder, after I almost, for those cursed hundred crowns, beat up many times this gentleman who happens today to be my father![11] But since Heaven has saved my virtues from these dangers, father of mine, please accept

[10] *End of the deletion.*
[11] *An allusion to Figaro's successful swindle of a hundred crowns from Bartholo. See* The Barber of Seville.

my apologies . . . And you, mother of mine, kiss me . . . as maternally as you can. (MARCELINE *clasps him about the neck.*)

SCENE 17

BARTHOLO, FIGARO, MARCELINE, BRID'OISON,
SUZANNE, ANTONIO, THE COUNT

SUZANNE: (*running with a purse in her hand*) My lord, stop. Do not marry them: I've come to pay this with the dowry my mistress has given me.

COUNT: (*aside*) The devil take your mistress! It seems that everything is conspiring . . . (*Exit*)

SCENE 18

BARTHOLO, ANTONIO, SUZANNE, FIGARO,
MARCELINE, BRID'OISON

ANTONIO: (*seeing* FIGARO *embracing his mother, says to* SUZANNE) Payment, eh! I see, I see.

SUZANNE: (*turns around*) I've seen enough; let's go, uncle.

FIGARO: (*stopping her*) Please don't. What is it you've seen?

SUZANNE: My weakness of mind and your cowardice.

FIGARO: Neither of them.

SUZANNE: (*angry*) And your willingness to marry her, since you caress her.

FIGARO: (*gayly*) I caress her, but I don't marry her. (SUZANNE *wants to leave;* FIGARO *holds her back.*)

SUZANNE: (*slaps him*) You are quite impertinent to dare to hold me back.

FIGARO: (*to the company*) Is that love? Before you leave us, I beg of you, take a good look at that dear woman.

SUZANNE: I'm looking at her.

FIGARO: And she strikes you?

SUZANNE: As hideous.

FIGARO: Long live jealousy! it spares no pains.

MARCELINE: (*with open arms*) Come embrace your mother, my pretty Suzannette. The naughty fellow who is tormenting you is my son.

SUZANNE (*runs to her*) You, his mother! (*They remain clasped in each other's arms.*)

ANTONIO: It must have just happened.

FIGARO: Only just now.

MARCELINE: (*with fervor*) No, my heart strongly drawn to him was mistaken only as to its reason. Blood was speaking to me.

FIGARO: And good sense to me, mother of mine, which served me as an instinct when I refused you, for I was far from hating you; witness the money . . .

MARCELINE: (*hands him a paper*) It is yours; take back your note, it is your dowry.

SUZANNE: (*throws him the purse*) And take this one also.

FIGARO: Many thanks.

MARCELINE: (*excited*) Unfortunate as a girl, I was about to become the most wretched of wives, and now I am the happiest of mothers! Come kiss me, my two children; all my feelings are centered upon you. As happy as anyone can be, oh! children, how I am going to love!

FIGARO: (*moved and speaking hastily*) Please stop, dear mother, please stop! Do you want to see my eyes dissolve away in the first tears they know? They are tears of joy, at least. But what a fool I've been, I almost felt ashamed of them as I felt them drop on my hands. Look (*he shows his fingers outspread*); and I was stupidly holding them back! Away, shame! I want to laugh and cry at the same time. What I feel does not come twice to a man. (*He embraces his mother on one side of him, and* SUZANNE *on the other.*[12])

MARCELINE: Oh, my dear!

SUZANNE: My very dear!

BRID'OISON: (*wiping his eyes with a handkerchief*) Very well, I'm a f-fool too!

FIGARO: (*excited*) Grief, I can now defy you! Reach me, if you dare, between these two women I love.

ANTONIO: (*to* FIGARO) Not so much blarney, please.

[12] *Beaumarchais's note: Bartholo, Antonio, Suzanne, Figaro, Marceline, Brid'oison.*

Apropos of marriage in good families, that of the parents is supposed to precede. Do yours ask each other's hand?

BARTHOLO: May my hand shrivel up and fall off if ever I give it to the mother of such a character!

ANTONIO: (*to* BARTHOLO) So you're only an unnatural father? (*To* FIGARO.) In that case, our Lothario, there's no longer any bargain.

SUZANNE: Oh, uncle! . . .

ANTONIO: Shall I give my sister's child to this here who's nobody's child?

BRID'OISON: How c-can that be, idiot? One is always somebody's child.

ANTONIO: Nonsense! . . . he shan't have her anyhow.
(*Exit.*)

SCENE 19

BARTHOLO, SUZANNE, FIGARO,
MARCELINE, BRID'OISON

BARTHOLO: (*to* FIGARO) Better look for somebody to adopt you. (*He wants to go.*)

MARCELINE: (*running to seize* BARTHOLO *around the middle, pulls him back*) Stop, doctor, don't go!

FIGARO: (*aside*) No, all the fools of Andalusia are, I believe, rabid against my poor marriage!

SUZANNE:[13] (*to* BARTHOLO) Dear little father, he is your son.

[13] *Beaumarchais's note: Suzanne, Bartholo, Marceline, Figaro, Brid'oison.*

MARCELINE: He has wit, talent, presence.

FIGARO: (*to* BARTHOLO) And he never cost you a penny.

BARTHOLO: What about the hundred crowns he robbed me of?

MARCELINE: (*fondling him*) We'll take such good care of you, papa!

SUZANNE: (*fondling him*) We'll love you so much, dear little papa!

BARTHOLO: (*moved*) Papa! dear papa! dear little papa! now I'm going to be an even bigger fool than this gentleman. (*Pointing to* BRID'OISON.) I'm being led like a child. (MARCELINE *and* SUZANNE *embrace him.*) Oh, no, I haven't said yes. (*He turns around.*) What's become of my lord?

FIGARO: Let's run and join him; let's force a decision from him. If he thought up some new scheme, we would have to begin all over again.

ALL TOGETHER: Let's go, let's go. (*They drag* BARTHOLO *outside.*)

SCENE 20

BRID'OISON: (*alone*) "An even bigger fool than this gentleman." One can say that s-sort of thing about oneself, but . . . They're not at all polite in this p-place. (*Exit.*)

ACT FOUR

The stage represents a large room bedecked with lighted candelabra, flowers, garlands, indicative of preparations for a party. Downstage, to the right, is a writing table, behind which there is an armchair.

SCENE I

FIGARO, SUZANNE

FIGARO: (*holding her around the waist*) Very well, love, are you happy? She converted her doctor, didn't she, my silver-tongued mother! In spite of his reluctance, he is marrying and your churlish uncle can't help himself. Only my lord is in a rage; for, after all, our marriage will become the price for theirs. Why don't you laugh a little at this fine outcome?

SUZANE: Have you seen anything odder?

FIGARO: Or rather so jolly. All we wanted was a dowry, squeezed out of His Excellency; now we have two which do not come from him. A persistent rival was hounding you; I was being tormented by a fury! all that has been changed for us in the *best* of mothers. Yesterday I was, so to speak, alone in the world; today I have all my relatives. True, they're not so magnificent as I had imagined them, but good enough for us, who haven't the ambition of the rich.

SUZANNE: Yet none of the things you had planned and we expected, my dear, came through.

FIGARO: Chance did a better job than all of us, my sweet. That's the way of the world. You toil, you scheme, you plan in one corner; Fortune performs in another. From the ravenous conqueror who would like to swallow the earth to the peaceful blind man who lets himself be led by his dog, all are the playthings of fate's whims; indeed, the blind man is often better led by his dog, less deceived in his opinions than the other man with his retinue. As for that lovable blind fellow called Love . . . (*He again seizes her tenderly about the waist.*)

SUZANNE: Ah! he's the only one who interests me!

FIGARO: Well, let me be the good dog in Folly's employ who leads him to your darling little door, and there we'll live cosily for the rest of our lives.

SUZANNE: (*laughing*) Love and you?

FIGARO: I and Love.

SUZANNE: And you won't look for other lodgings?

FIGARO: If you catch me at it, I'm willing that a hundred million gallants . . .

SUZANNE: You're going to exaggerate: tell me the honest truth.

FIGARO: My truest truth!

SUZANNE: Shame on you, rogue! Are there several?

FIGARO: Oh, yes! Ever since it has been observed that

with the passing of time old follies become wisdom, and that early little lies, rather poorly planted, have produced great big truths, there have been endless kinds of truths. There are those one dare not proclaim, for every truth is not fit to say; and there are those one brags about without placing faith in them, for every truth is not fit to believe. And how about passionate oaths, mothers' threats, drinkers' resolutions, office holders' promises, businessmen's final offers: there is no end. Only my love for my Suzy is the real truth.

SUZANNE: I like your gaiety because it is wild; it shows that you are happy. But let's speak of the meeting with the Count.

FIGARO: Or better, let's not speak of that ever; it nearly cost me Suzanne.

SUZANNE: You don't want it any longer to take place?

FIGARO: If you love me, Suzy, your word of honor on this. Let him get a chill, it'll be his punishment.

SUZANNE: It cost me more to agree to it than I have distress in giving it up; I'll never mention it again.

FIGARO: Your truest truth?

SUZANNE: I'm not like you learned people; I have only one truth.

FIGARO: And you'll love me a little bit?

SUZANNE: A great deal.

FIGARO: It's hardly enough.

SUZANNE: And why?

FIGARO: Why, in love, you see, too much is not even enough.

SUZANNE: I do not understand all these subtleties, but I'll love only my husband.

FIGARO: Keep your word and you will represent a fine exception to the rule. (*He wants to kiss her.*)

SCENE 2

FIGARO, SUZANNE, THE COUNTESS

COUNTESS: I was right when I said: wherever they happen to be, you may be sure they are together. Come now, Figaro, anytime you're indulging in a tête-à-tête you're robbing the future, marriage, and yourself. People are waiting for you and getting impatient.

FIGARO: It's true, madam, I was forgetting myself. I'm going to show them my excuse. (*He wants to take* SUZANNE *with him.*)

COUNTESS: (*holds her back*) She'll follow you.

SCENE 3

SUZANNE, THE COUNTESS

COUNTESS: Have you what's needed to change clothes?

SUZANNE: Nothing is needed, madam; the meeting is off.

COUNTESS: Ah! you have changed your mind?

SUZANNE: It's Figaro.

COUNTESS: You are deceiving me.

SUZANNE: Good Heavens!

COUNTESS: Figaro is not a man to let a dowry slip from his hands.

SUZANNE: Oh, madam, what can you be thinking?

COUNTESS: That finally in agreement with the Count, you are now sorry you confided his plans to me. I know you like a book. Leave me. (*She wants to leave.*)

SUZANNE: (*kneels down*) In the name of Heaven, hope of all, you cannot know, madam, the wrong you do Suzanne! After you've been so endlessly kind to me, and the dowry you've given me! . . .

COUNTESS: (*lifts her up*) But, of course . . . I don't know what I'm saying! Since you are changing places with me, dear heart, you won't be going into the garden. You'll be keeping your word to your husband and helping me to bring mine back.

SUZANNE: Oh how you grieved me!

COUNTESS: I am a thoughtless woman. (*She kisses her on the forehead.*) Where is your meeting place?

SUZANNE: (*kisses her hand*) I heard only the word "garden."

COUNTESS: (*pointing to the table*) Take that pen and let's name a spot.

SUZANNE: I, write to him!

COUNTESS: You must.

SUZANNE: But at least, madam, you . . .

COUNTESS: I'll vouch for everything. (SUZANNE *sits, the* COUNTESS *dictates*) "A new song to the tune of . . . 'How lovely it will be under the great chestnut trees tonight . . . How lovely it will be tonight . . .' "

SUZANNE: (*writes*) Under the great chestnuts . . . Nothing else?

COUNTESS: Do you fear he will not understand you?

SUZANNE: It's right. (*She folds the note.*) What kind of seal?

COUNTESS: A pin, quickly! it will serve as a reply. Write on the back: "Please return the seal."

SUZANNE: (*writes laughing*) Ha! "the seal"! . . . This one is funnier than the one on the officer's commission.

COUNTESS: (*in painful recollection*) Oh!

SUZANNE: (*looks on her person*) I haven't any pin, none!

COUNTESS: (*unpins the collar of her gown*) Take this one. (*The page's ribbon falls from her bosom to the ground.*) Oh, my ribbon!

SUZANNE: (*picks it up*) It's the little thief's? And you had the cruelty? . . .

COUNTESS: Could I let him wear it on his arm? A fine spectacle it would have been? Please give it back to me.

SUZANNE: Madam cannot wear it, spotted as it is with the young man's blood.

COUNTESS: (*takes it back*) It's excellent for Fanchette . . . when she next brings me a bouquet.

SCENE 4

A YOUNG SHEPHERDESS, CHÉRUBIN, *dressed as a girl;*
FANCHETTE *and* MANY YOUNG GIRLS *dressed like her
and carrying bouquets,* THE COUNTESS, SUZANNE

FANCHETTE: Madam, these are girls from the village that
come to bring you flowers.

COUNTESS: (*quickly hiding her ribbon*) They are charming! It grieves me, dears, not to know you all by name.
(*Pointing to* CHÉRUBIN.) Who is this lovely child who
looks so shy?

SHEPHERDESS: She's a cousin of mine, madam, who has
come only for the wedding.

COUNTESS: She's pretty. Since I can't wear twenty bouquets, let's honor the stranger. (*She takes* CHÉRUBIN's *bouquet and kisses him on the forehead.*) She's blushing. (*To*
SUZANNE.) Suzy, don't you think . . . she looks like someone we know?

SUZANNE: Really, I can hardly tell them apart.

CHÉRUBIN: (*aside, his hands on his heart*) Oh, that kiss
went through me!

THE GIRLS, CHÉRUBIN, *in the midst of them;* FAN-
CHETTE, ANTONIO, THE COUNT, THE COUNTESS, SU-
ZANNE

ANTONIO: And I tell you, my lord, he's here. They dressed him at my daughter's, all his clothes are still there, and here is his regulation hat, which I picked out of the package. (*He steps forward, and scanning the girls' faces, he recognizes* CHÉRUBIN, *takes off his female bonnet, which makes his long hair fall in ringlets. He puts the regulation hat on top.*) By gum, there's our officer!

COUNTESS: (*steps back*) Heavens!

SUZANNE: That young rogue!

ANTONIO: I was saying upstairs it was he! . . .

COUNT: (*angry*) Well, madam?

COUNTESS: Well, sir, you find me more surprised than you and at least as angry.

COUNT: Yes, but what about this morning?

COUNTESS: I should be guilty indeed if I kept up the deception any longer. He had dropped in to see me, and then we began the practical joke which these children have completed. You surprised us dressing him up. You are so quick tempered that he ran away, I got disturbed, and general fright did the rest.

COUNT: (*with rancor to* CHÉRUBIN) Why haven't you left?

CHÉRUBIN: (*flinging off his hat*) My lord . . .

COUNT: I'll punish you for disobeying.

FANCHETTE: (*thoughtlessly*) Oh, my lord, listen to me. Every time you come to embrace me, you certainly know you always say: "Fanchette, dear, if you will love me, I'll give you anything you want."

COUNT: (*blushing*) I have said that?

FANCHETTE: Yes, my lord. Instead of punishing Chérubin, give him to me for a husband, and I'll love you madly.

COUNT: (*aside*) Captivated by a page!

COUNTESS: Very well, sir, it is your time now. This child's confession, as naïve as mine, bears witness to a double truth: that when I cause you worry it is always unintentional, whereas you do all you can to increase and justify my own.

ANTONIO: You too, my lord? By gum! I'll get after her as I did her late mother, now gone . . . Not that it will result in anything, but madam surely knows that little girls when they're growing . . .

COUNT: (*abashed, aside*) There is an evil genius here who turns everything against me!

SCENE 6

THE GIRLS, CHÉRUBIN, ANTONIO, FIGARO,
THE COUNT, THE COUNTESS, SUZANNE

FIGARO: My lord, if you detain the young ladies, we can't begin the party or the dance.

COUNT: You, dance! you're not thinking of it. After this morning's fall, you sprained your right foot, remember?

FIGARO: (*moving his leg*) It's still a trifle sore; it's nothing. (*To the* GIRLS.) Come, darlings, come.

COUNT: (*turns* FIGARO *about*) You were very lucky the beds were only soft earth!

FIGARO: Very lucky, no doubt, otherwise . . .

ANTONIO: (*turns him around*) Then he curled up as he fell all the way down to the bottom.

FIGARO: A more clever man would have remained in the air, wouldn't he? (*To the* GIRLS.) Are you coming, ladies?

ANTONIO: (*turns* FIGARO *about*) And all the while the little page was galloping on his horse toward Seville?

FIGARO: Galloping, or perhaps sauntering! . . .

COUNT: (*turns* FIGARO *about*) And you had his commission in your pocket?

FIGARO: (*a bit surprised*) Assuredly, but why this inquiry? (*To the* GIRLS.) Come now, girls.

ANTONIO: (*pulling* CHÉRUBIN *by the arm*) Here's one who claims my future nephew is only a liar.

FIGARO: (*amazed*) Chérubin! . . . (*aside*) Plague take the little braggart!

ANTONIO: Have you understood it now?

FIGARO: (*searching*) I've understood it . . . I've understood it . . . By the way, what's his story?

COUNT: (*drily*) It's not a story, he says it was he who jumped into the stocks.

FIGARO: (*musing*) Well, if he says so . . . , that may be! I don't contradict what I don't know.

COUNT: So you and he?

FIGARO: Why not? The jumping fever is catching: think of Panurge's[1] sheep. And when you are angry, no one would not prefer to risk . . .

COUNT: How, two at a time . . .

FIGARO: We'd have jumped by the dozen; and what difference does it make, my lord, since no one was hurt? (*To the* GIRLS.) Now then, are you coming or aren't you?

COUNT: (*outraged*) Are we playing a farce? (*A prelude of a musical flourish can be heard.*)

FIGARO: There's the signal of the march. Fall in, my beauties, fall in. Come, Suzanne, give me your arm. (*Exeunt except* CHÉRUBIN, *his head hanging down.*)

[1] *Panurge, a character in Rabelais's* Pantagruel, *who induced all the sheep to jump overboard by throwing over the first one.*

SCENE 7

CHÉRUBIN, THE COUNT, THE COUNTESS

COUNT: (*watching* FIGARO *going off*) Did you ever see greater nerve? (*To the page.*) As for you, Mister Sly Boots, who pretend to be ashamed, go and dress yourself very quickly and let me not see your face for the rest of the evening.

COUNTESS: He is going to be awfully bored.

CHÉRUBIN: (*thoughtlessly*) Bored! I carry on my brow enough happiness to outweigh more than a hundred years in jail. (*He puts on his hat and leaves.*)

SCENE 8

THE COUNT, THE COUNTESS

(*The* COUNTESS *fans herself violently without talking.*)

COUNT: What is so happy about his brow?

COUNTESS: (*embarrassed*) His . . . first officer's hat, I suppose. With children everything is like a toy.

COUNT: You're not staying, Countess?

COUNTESS: You know I don't feel well.

COUNT: One moment for the sake of your protégée, or I'll think you are angry.

COUNTESS: Here are the two wedding processions, let us sit down and receive them.

COUNT: (*aside*) The wedding! Well, one must endure what one can't prevent. (*The* COUNT *and the* COUNTESS *sit to one side of the room.*)

SCENE 9

THE COUNT, THE COUNTESS, *sitting; enter the processions with the* FOLIES D'ESPAGNE *played to a march tempo*

MARCH

GAMEKEEPERS, *muskets on their shoulders.*

THE JUSTICE of *Aguas-Frescas,* THE ALDERMEN, BRID'-OISON.

THE PEASANTS AND THEIR WOMEN *in holiday dress.*

TWO GIRLS *carrying the virgin's bonnet with white feathers.*

TWO OTHERS, *the white veil.*

TWO OTHERS, *the gloves and the corsage.*

ANTONIO *gives* SUZANNE *his hand, being the one who will give her away to* FIGARO.

OTHER GIRLS *carry another bonnet, another veil, another white corsage, similar to the first, for* MARCELINE.

FIGARO *gives his hand to* MARCELINE, *being the one who will give her away to the* DOCTOR, *who brings up the rear* of the procession, *wearing a large boutonniere. The* GIRLS, *as they pass before the* COUNT, *deliver to his* VALETS *all the paraphernalia destined for* SUZANNE *and* MARCELINE.

THE PEASANTS, *men and women, forming two lines on each side of the salon, dance a fandango (a well-known tune) to an accompaniment of castanets. Then the orchestra plays the refrain of the duet, during which* ANTONIO *takes* SUZANNE *to the* COUNT. *She kneels before him, he puts the bonnet and the veil on her, and gives her the bouquet. Two* GIRLS *sing the following duet. (A well-known tune.)*

> Sing, young bride, the glorious benefaction
> Of a master who has displaced his lust;
> He prefers to pleasure a noble action,
> And to your husband he hands you chaste and pure.

SUZANNE *is kneeling; and, as the duet concludes, she tugs at the* COUNT's *cloak and shows him the note she has. She then puts her hand, which faces the spectators, to her hair, or the* COUNT *seems to adjust her bonnet; she gives him the note.*

THE COUNT *puts the note furtively inside his breast while the duet ends, the fiancée rises, and makes a low curtsy.*

FIGARO *comes to receive her from the hands of the* COUNT *and steps back with her to the other side of the salon, near* MARCELINE. *(There is meanwhile another reprise of the fandango.)*

THE COUNT, *in haste to read what he has received, comes downstage and pulls the paper from his breast; but in tak-*

ing it out, he makes the gesture of a man who has cruelly pricked his finger; he shakes it, squeezes it, licks it. He looks at the paper fastened with a pin and says:

COUNT: (*While he and* FIGARO *speak, the orchestra plays pianissimo.*) The deuce with women who stick pins everywhere! (*He throws it on the ground, then reads the note and kisses it.*)

FIGARO: (*who has seen everything, says to his mother and* SUZANNE) It's a billet-doux that some little hussy must have slipped into his hand as she passed by. It was sealed with a pin that terribly pricked him. (*The dance resumes. The* COUNT, *who has read the note, turns it over and sees the request to return the pin as a reply. He looks on the ground, finally finds the pin, and sticks it in his sleeve.*)

FIGARO: (*to* SUZANNE *and* MARCELINE) From the beloved anything is dear. So he's retrieving the pin. What a queer fish he is! (*Meanwhile,* SUZANNE *has been exchanging signs of intelligence with the* COUNTESS. *The dance ends and the refrain of the duet is played again.*) (FIGARO *takes* MARCELINE *to the* COUNT, *just as* SUZANNE *has been taken, at the precise moment when the* COUNT *takes the bonnet and when the duet is about to begin, the proceedings are interrupted by the following cries:*)

USHER: (*shouting at the door*) Keep back, gentlemen, you can't all get in. Help here! the guards! the guards! (*The guards go quickly toward the door.*)

COUNT: (*rising*) What is the matter?

USHER: My lord, it is Master Bazile who is surrounded by the whole village because he sings as he walks.

COUNT: Let him enter alone.

COUNTESS: Order me to withdraw.

COUNT: I shan't forget your obliging me.

COUNTESS: Suzanne? . . . She will be back. (*Aside, to* SUZANNE.) Let's go change our clothes. (*Exeunt.*)

MARCELINE: He never shows up but to do harm.

FIGARO: Ah! I'm going to change his tune!

SCENE 10

ALL THE PRECEDING ACTORS, *except the Countess and Suzanne;* BAZILE, *holding his guitar;* GRIPPE-SOLEIL

BAZILE: (*enters singing to the tune of the final song of the play*)

A well-known tune
Sensitive and faithful hearts,
Who blame all love's wanderings,
Cease launching your angry darts;
Is it a crime for one to change?
For if Cupid carries wings,
Is it not to flit and range?
Is it not to flit and range?
Is it not to flit and range?

FIGARO: (*goes toward him*) Yes, it's for that precisely

that Love has wings. Friend, what do you mean by this song?

BAZILE: (*pointing to* GRIPPE-SOLEIL) I mean that after proving my submission to my lord and entertaining this gentleman, who is of his company, I can in turn claim his justice.

GRIPPE-SOLEIL: Pooh! my lord! he didn't entertain me at all, with his bits of tunes.

COUNT: Well, what is it you want, Bazile?

BAZILE: What belongs to me, my lord, Marceline's hand; and I come to oppose . . .

FIGARO: (*draws close*) Has it been a long time since you saw the face of a lunatic?

BAZILE: Sir, this very moment.

FIGARO: Since my eyes serve you so well as a mirror, study in it the effect of my prophecy. If you so much as show that you come near madam . . .

BARTHOLO: (*laughing*) But why? Let him speak.

BRID'OISON: (*comes forward between them*) M-must two friends . . . ?

FIGARO: We, friends?

BAZILE: Ridiculous!

FIGARO: (*quickly*) Because he writes dull church music?

BAZILE: (*quickly*) And he writes newspaper verse?

FIGARO: (*quickly*) A tavern musician!

BAZILE: (*quickly*) A gazette drudge!

FIGARO: (*quickly*) An oratorio-monger!

BAZILE: (*quickly*) A diplomatic jockey!

COUNT: (*sitting*) Impudent both of you!

BAZILE: He's failed me at every turn.

FIGARO: Well said, if it were true!

BAZILE: Saying everywhere that I'm an ass.

FIGARO: You take me for an echo of public opinion?

BAZILE: While there's no talented singer I haven't trained.

FIGARO: Strained.

BAZILE: He repeats his insults!

FIGARO: And why not, if it's true? Are you a prince that you should be flattered? Endure truth, villain, since you can't be a liar, or if you fear the truth will come from us, why do you come to interrupt our wedding celebration?

BAZILE: (*to* MARCELINE) Did you or did you not promise me that if you weren't provided for within four years, you would give me preference?

MARCELINE: Under what condition did I make the promise?

BAZILE: That if you found a certain lost child, I would adopt him out of kindness.

ALL: (*together*) He's been found!

BAZILE: That need be no obstacle!

ALL: (*together, pointing to* FIGARO) There he is!

BAZILE: (*shrinking back with terror*) Get thee behind me!

BRID'OISON: Does that mean that you g-give up his d-dear mother!

BAZILE: What can be worse than to be thought the father of such a scamp?

FIGARO: Why, to be thought your son; you're making fun of me!

BAZILE: (*pointing to* FIGARO) The moment this gentleman is somebody here, I declare I'm no longer a part of it. (*Exit.*)

SCENE 11

THE PRECEDING ACTORS, *except Bazile*

BARTHOLO: (*laughing*) Ha! ha! ha! ha!

FIGARO: (*leaping for joy*) At last I'll have my bride!

COUNT: (*aside*) And I my mistress. (*He rises.*)

BRID'OISON: (*to* MARCELINE) And everybody is s-satisfied.

COUNT: Let the two marriage contracts be drawn up, I shall sign them.

ALL: (*together*) Hurrah! (*Exeunt.*)

COUNT: I need some time to myself. (*He wants to leave with the others.*)

SCENE 12

GRIPPE-SOLEIL, FIGARO, MARCELINE, THE COUNT

GRIPPE-SOLEIL: (*to* FIGARO) Now I'm going to help set up the fireworks under the great chestnuts as I was told.

COUNT: (*comes back running*) What fool gave you such an order?

FIGARO: Where's the harm?

COUNT: (*with animation*) Why, the Countess is indisposed. Where can she see the fireworks unless it's on the terrace, opposite her room?

FIGARO: You understand, Grippe-Soleil? On the terrace.

COUNT: Under the great chestnuts! a fine idea! (*Leaving, aside.*) They were going to set fire to my meeting place.

SCENE 13

FIGARO, MARCELINE

FIGARO: How much considerateness for his wife! (*He wants to leave.*)

MARCELINE: (*stops him*) A word with you, my son. I owe you an apology. A misdirected feeling made me unjust to your charming wife; I thought she was in league with the

Count, although Bazile had told me that she always rejected his advances.

FIGARO: You don't know your son well if you believe that female impulses can shake him. I defy the cleverest to delude me.

MARCELINE: It's always fortunate to think so, my son; jealousy . . .

FIGARO: . . . Is only a stupid child of pride, or it's a madman's disease. Oh, I have on this point, mother, an imperturbable philosophy. So even if Suzanne should deceive me some day, I'll forgive her in advance; she will have worked long . . . (*He turns around and sees* FAN-CHETTE, *who is looking everywhere.*)

SCENE 14

FIGARO, FANCHETTE, MARCELINE

FIGARO: So-o-o, little cousin! You're listening to us!

FANCHETTE: Oh, no! They say it isn't proper.

FIGARO: That's true; but as it's useful, it's often considered worth the trouble.

FANCHETTE: I was looking to see if somebody was here.

FIGARO: Already so full of guile, you rascal! you know perfectly well he can't be here.

FANCHETTE: And who, pray?

FIGARO: Chérubin.

FANCHETTE: It isn't he that I'm looking for, I know very well where he is. It's cousin Suzanne.

FIGARO: And what does my little cousin want from her?

FANCHETTE: You, my little cousin, I can tell. It is . . . it's only a pin I want to give her.

FIGARO: (*sharply*) A pin! a pin! . . . and from whom, you hussy? At your age you're already in a business . . . (*He catches himself and says gently.*) You already do very well whatever you do, Fanchette; and my pretty cousin is so obliging . . .

FANCHETTE: Why did I make him angry? I'm going.

FIGARO: (*stopping her*) Don't go, don't. I was only teasing. Listen: that little pin of yours is the one that my lord told you to deliver to Suzanne, the one that served to fasten a little paper he had in his hand; you see I know what I'm talking about.

FANCHETTE: Why ask when you know it so well?

FIGARO: (*fumbling*) It's because it's rather funny to know how my lord went about sending you on your errand.

FANCHETTE: (*naïvely*) He did it almost as you say: "Here, little Fanchette, give back this pin to your beautiful cousin; just tell her it's the seal for the big chestnuts."

FIGARO: "The big—?

FANCHETTE: "—chestnuts." It is true he added: "Be careful no one sees you."

FIGARO: Well, cousin, you must obey and luckily no one has seen you. Run your pretty errand and don't tell Suzanne a word more than my lord has ordered.

FANCHETTE: And why should I say more? He takes me for a child, my cousin. (*She goes out skipping.*)

SCENE 15

FIGARO, MARCELINE

FIGARO: Well, mother?

MARCELINE: Well, my son?

FIGARO: (*as if choking*) For this man! . . . Some things really are too much! . . .

MARCELINE: Some things, of course! What's wrong?

FIGARO: (*his hands on his chest*) What I've just heard, mother, weighs on me like lead—here.

MARCELINE: Your assured face of a while ago was only an inflated balloon? a pin has made everything collapse!

FIGARO: (*furious*) But that pin, mother, was the one he picked up! . . .

MARCELINE: (*recalling his words*) "Jealousy! Oh, I have on this point, mother, an imperturbable philosophy . . . ; so even if Suzanne should deceive me, I'll forgive her . . ."

FIGARO: (*with animation*) Oh, mother, one speaks as one feels at the time: let the coolest judge plead his own case and see how he explains the law! I am no longer astonished that he was so angry about those fireworks!—As for my darling with fine pins, she hasn't got where she is, chestnut trees or no chestnut trees! If my marriage is enough to warrant my anger, on the other hand, it isn't enough for me to drop one wife and marry another . . .

MARCELINE: A fine conclusion! Let's spoil everything on a mere suspicion! How do you know, tell me, it's you she's deceiving and not the Count? Have you studied her anew to condemn her without appeal? Do you know whether she will go under the trees, or what her intention is, or what she will say and do if she goes? I thought you had more judgment!

FIGARO: (*kissing her hand with respect*) My mother is right, she is right, right, always right! But, mamma, let's grant something to natural impulses; one feels better afterwards. Now let's examine before accusing and acting. I know where the meeting is to be. Farewell, mother! (*Exit.*)

SCENE 16

MARCELINE: (*alone*) Farewell. And I too know where it is. After stopping him, let's look after Suzanne, or rather, let's warn her. She is such a pretty creature! Ah! when our own interest does not divide us, we women are all inclined to uphold our poor, downtrodden sex against the proved, terrifying . . . (*laughing*) and yet somewhat dull-witted masculine sex. (*Exit.*)

ACT FIVE

The stage represents a stand of chestnut trees in a park; two pavilions, kiosks or garden temples occupy the right and the left; behind is a decorated clearing; in front a lawn with seats. The theatre is dark.

SCENE I

FANCHETTE: (*alone, holding in one hand two small cakes and an orange; in the other, a lighted paper lantern*) The pavilion on the left, he said. This must be the one. But suppose my fine fellow were not to show up . . . Those terrible kitchen people wouldn't even give me an orange and two cookies! "For whom, miss?" "Well, sir, it's for someone." "Oh, we know." And if that were the case; just because my lord doesn't want to see him, must he starve? All the same, it cost me a big kiss on the cheek! . . . Who knows, perhaps he'll pay for it. (*She sees* FIGARO, *who comes to identify her. She cries out.*) Ah! . . . (*She runs away and enters the pavilion to her left.*)

SCENE 2

FIGARO, *with a large cloak on his shoulders and a broad-brimmed hat;* BAZILE, ANTONIO, BARTHOLO, BRID'OISON, GRIPPE-SOLEIL, A GROUP OF VALETS AND WORKMEN

FIGARO: (*alone at first*) It's Fanchette! (*He scans the others as they arrive and says roughly:*) Good day, gentlemen, good evening. Are you all here?

BAZILE: All those you urged to come.

FIGARO: About what time is it?

ANTONIO: (*glances upward*) The moon should be up.

BARTHOLO: Well, what black arts are you getting ready for? He looks like a conspirator.

FIGARO: (*getting excited*) Isn't it for a wedding, tell me, that you're gathered at the castle?

BRID'OISON: C-certainly.

ANTONIO: We were going over yonder, in the park, to wait for the signal to begin the festivities.

FIGARO: You shan't go a step further, gentlemen. It's here, under the chestnuts, that we're going to celebrate the respectable fiancée I am marrying and the faithful lord who has destined her for himself.

BAZILE: (*recalling the day's occurrences*) Ah, yes. I know all about it. Let's withdraw, if you please: it's the matter of a rendezvous. I'll tell you about it later.

BRID'OISON: (*to* FIGARO) We'll c-come back.

FIGARO: When you hear me call, don't fail to run up all of you and curse Figaro if he doesn't show you a fine spectacle.

BARTHOLO: Remember that a wise man does not start a quarrel with the great.

FIGARO: I'll remember.

BARTHOLO: They have a great advantage over us, thanks to their rank.

FIGARO: To say nothing of their perseverance, which you're forgetting. But remember also that once a man is known to be timid, he's at the mercy of every scoundrel.

BARTHOLO: Well said.

FIGARO: And among my names is Verte-Allure, on my mother's side.

BARTHOLO: He has a devil within him.

BRID'OISON: T-that he has.

BAZILE: (*aside*) The Count and Suzanne have planned this without me? I'm not sorry for this escapade.

FIGARO: (*to the* VALETS) You rascals, do as I told you: light up all the surroundings or in the name of Death, which I would like to throttle, when I grab one of you by the arm . . . (*He shakes* GRIPPE-SOLEIL's *arm.*)

GRIPPE-SOLEIL: (*goes off shouting and weeping.* Ah, oh, ah, oh, perish the brute!

BAZILE: (*leaving*) Heaven give you joy, young newly-wed! (*Exeunt.*)

SCENE 3

FIGARO: (*alone, pacing to and fro in the dark, says in the most sombre tone*) Oh, woman, woman, woman! weak and deceitful creature! . . . No animal on earth can go against instinct; is it yours to deceive? After refusing me stubbornly when I urged her before her mistress, in the very moment she gives me her word, in the very midst of the ceremony . . . He was laughing as he read, the villain! and I, like a booby! . . . No, my lord Count, you shan't have her . . . you shan't have her! . . . Because you are a great lord you think you are a great genius! . . . Nobility, wealth, a station, emoluments: all that makes one so proud! What have you done to earn so many honors? You took the trouble to be born, that's all; apart from that, you're a rather ordinary man! Whereas I, by Heaven! lost in the nameless herd, I had to exert more knowledge and skill merely to survive than has been spent in a hundred years in governing the Spanish Empire: and you want to joust! . . . Someone's coming . . . it's she! . . . No, it's no one. The night is pitch dark and here I am plying the foolish trade of husband, although I'm only half of one! (*He sits down on a bench.*) Can there be anything stranger than my destiny! The son of God knows whom, stolen by bandits, brought up in their ways, I become disgusted with them and want to lead an honest life; and everywhere I am repulsed! I learn chemistry, pharmacy, surgery, and all the influence of a great lord can scarcely secure me a veterinary's lancet!—Weary of making sick animals gloomier and in the hope of doing the opposite, I go headlong for the stage; far better if I had hung a stone around my neck! I write a play satirizing harem life. Being a Spanish author, I believe I can criticize Mohammed without scruple; instantly an emissary . . . from God knows where complains that my verses offend the Sublime Porte, Persia, part of the Indian peninsula, all Egypt, the kingdoms of Barca, Tripoli, Tunis, Algeria, and Morocco: and my play is done for, to please the Mohammedan princes, not one of whom, I believe, can read, and all of whom brand us on the scapula and call us "Christian dogs." Not being able to degrade the mind, one takes revenge by abusing it.—My cheeks were getting hollow; my rent had fallen due; I could see from afar the terrible bailiff with a pen stuck in his wig, so I shudder and exert myself anew. A debate arises about the nature of riches, and since it isn't necessary to own something to argue about it, being penniless, I write on the value of money and interest. Soon I find myself inside a coach looking at the drawbridge of a prison, entering which, I left hope and freedom behind. (*He gets up.*) How I should like to hold one of these potentates who last four days in office, so ready to mete out punishment, when a healthy disfavor has sobered his pride! I should tell him . . . that printed nonsense is important only in countries where its free circulation is hindered; that without the freedom to criticize, there can be no flattering praise, that only petty men fear petty writings. (*He sits down.*) Weary of feeding an obscure guest, one day they threw me out into the street; and since a man must eat even if he's no longer in jail, I sharpen my quill and ask people what is in the news: I'm told that during my retreat at public expense, there has been established in Madrid a system of free trade, which extends even to a free press, and that, provided I do not write about the government, or about religion, or politics, or ethics, or people in power or with influence, or the Opera, or other theatres, or about anybody connected with something, I can print whatever I choose under the supervision of two or three censors. To take advantage of this sweet liberty, I launch a periodical, and believing I poach on no one else's preserves, I call it *The Useless Journal.* Ugh! I see a thousand poor devils of hacks rise against me. I am suppressed and once again without a job.—Despair was about to seize me when someone thought of me for a vacant position, but unfortunately I was suited to it: they needed an accountant but a dancer got the job. All that was left was to steal. I became a faro[1] croupier: ah, then, my dear people! I dine out and persons known as the right persons courteously open their houses to me, keeping for themselves three quarters of the take. I could have recouped my losses; I had even begun to un-

[1] *"Faro" was a popular card game of the eighteenth century. In this game the players bet against the dealer as to the order in which certain cards will appear. The dealing is from a box, and the cards are dealt by twos from a pack of fifty-two.*

derstand that to earn money, know-how is better than knowledge. But everyone around me robbed left and right while requiring that I remain honest, I had to go under again. For the moment I was about to leave the world— twenty fathoms of water were going to separate me from it —when a beneficent God recalled me to my original trade. I take my case and my English leather and leave the smoke of glory to the fools that feed on it. With it, I leave behind shame, which is too heavy a load for a pedestrian to bear, I go from town to town shaving people, and I live at last a life without care. A great lord passes through Seville; he recognizes me, I marry him off, and as a reward for my services in obtaining a wife, he wants to intercept mine! Thereupon, storms and intrigues. About to fall into an abyss, nearly married to my own mother, when lo! my relatives materialize. (*He rises and gets excited.*) There is a regular argument: "it's you, it's he, it's I; no, it isn't we": well, who then? (*He falls back into the seat.*) What an odd series of events? How did it happen to me? Why these things and not others? Who fixed them in my head? Forced to go through the road of life, not knowing where it leads and bound to leave it against my will, I have strewn it with as many flowers as my cheerfulness has permitted. Still I say my cheerfulness without knowing if it's mine any more than those other things: nor do I know who this I may be with which I am concerned: it's a shapeless collection of unknown parts, then a puny imbecile being, a playful little animal, a young man thirsting for pleasure, having a real zest for enjoying, plying any trade to live: master here, valet there, according to the whim of fortune, ambitious from vanity, industrious by necessity, but lazy . . . with delight! an orator in danger, a poet for relaxation, a musician when the occasion arises, a lover in mad fits: I've seen everything, done everything, used up everything. My illusion is shattered, my eyes are open only too well! . . . Oh, Suzy, Suzy, Suzy! how many torments you are giving me! I hear footsteps . . . People are coming. This is the crisis. (*He withdraws into the downstage wing to his right.*)

SCENE 4

FIGARO, THE COUNTESS, *dressed as Suzy;* SUZANNE, *dressed as the Countess;* MARCELINE

SUZANNE: (*in a low voice to the* COUNTESS) Yes, Marceline told me that Figaro would be here.

MARCELINE: And so he is; lower your voice.

SUZANNE: So the one's eavesdropping and the other's going to come for me; let's begin.

MARCELINE: Not to miss a word, I'm going to hide in the pavilion. (*She goes into the same pavilion as* FANCHETTE.)

SCENE 5

FIGARO, THE COUNTESS, SUZANNE

SUZANNE: (*aloud*) Madam is trembling! can she be cold?

COUNTESS: (*aloud*) The evening is damp, I am going in.

SUZANNE: (*aloud*) If madam doesn't need me, I should like to take the air for a moment under those trees.

COUNTESS: (*aloud*) You'll catch your death of cold.

SUZANNE: (*aloud*) I'm quite used to it.

FIGARO: (*aside*) Her death, my foot! (SUZANNE *retreats to a place near the wings, on the opposite side from* FI-GARO.)

SCENE 6

FIGARO, CHÉRUBIN, THE COUNT,
THE COUNTESS, SUZANNE

(FIGARO *and* SUZANNE *retired on each side downstage.*)

CHÉRUBIN: (*dressed as an officer, arrives merrily singing the words of his ballad*)

> Tra-la-la-la-la
> A godmother had I,
> Whom always I adored.

COUNTESS: (*aside*) The little page!

CHÉRUBIN: (*stops*) People are walking here; let me take to my refuge, where little Fanchette . . . Oh, it's a woman!

COUNTESS: (*listens*) Oh, great Heavens!

CHÉRUBIN: (*stoops and glances from afar*) Can I be mistaken? That hat with feathers outlined against the sky looks to me like Suzy's.

COUNTESS: (*aside*) Suppose the Count were to appear! . . . (*The* COUNT *enters from the rear.*)

CHÉRUBIN: (*draws near and takes the* COUNTESS's *hand, which she pulls away*) Yes, it is that adorable girl named Suzanne. Could I be mistaken at the softness of this hand, or that slight trembling, or above all the beating of my own heart! (*He wants to put the back of the* COUNTESS's *hand against his heart, but she withdraws it.*)

COUNTESS: (*in a low voice*) Go away.

CHÉRUBIN: Could pity alone have led you purposely in this spot in the park where I've been hiding for a little while!

COUNTESS: Figaro is coming.

COUNT: (*coming forward, aside*) Isn't that Suzanne I see?

CHÉRUBIN: (*to the* COUNTESS) I do not fear Figaro at all and it's not he that you're waiting for.

COUNTESS: Who then?

COUNT: (*aside*) She is with somebody.

CHÉRUBIN: It's my lord, hussy, who asked you this morning for this rendezvous when I was behind the chair.

COUNT: (*aside, furious*) It's that infernal page again!

FIGARO: (*aside*) And they say one mustn't eavesdrop!

SUZANNE: (*aside*) The little chatterbox!

COUNTESS: (*to the page*) Be so kind as to go away.

CHÉRUBIN: Not at least without a reward for my obedience.

COUNTESS: (*frightened*) You claim? . . .

CHÉRUBIN: (*with fire*) Twenty kisses on your account first, and then one hundred for your fair mistress.

COUNTESS: You would dare?

CHÉRUBIN: Oh, yes, I would! You're taking her place with my lord, I take his with you. The one most tricked is Figaro.

FIGARO: (*aside*) That rascal!

SUZANNE: (*aside*) As brazen as a page. (CHÉRUBIN *wants to kiss the* COUNTESS. *The* COUNT *comes between them and receives the kiss.*)

COUNTESS: (*retreating*) Oh, Heavens!

FIGARO: (*aside, hearing the kiss*) It's a pretty hussy I'm marrying! (*He listens.*)

CHÉRUBIN: (*feeling the* COUNT's *clothes; aside*) It's my lord. (*He flees into the pavilion, into which* FANCHETTE *and* MARCELINE *have gone.*)

SCENE 7

FIGARO, THE COUNT, THE COUNTESS, SUZANNE

FIGARO: (*approaches*) I'm going . . .

COUNT: (*thinks he is talking to the page*) Since you do not repeat the kiss . . . (*He believes he is giving him a slap.*)

FIGARO: (*who is within range, receives it*) Ouch!

COUNT: . . . The first one's paid off, anyway.

FIGARO: (*aside, retreats and rubs his cheek*) This eavesdropping isn't all gain.

SUZANNE: (*laughing aloud on the other side*) Ha! ha! ha! ha!

COUNT: (*to the* COUNTESS, *whom he mistakes for* SUZANNE) I can't understand that page! He gets slapped very soundly and runs off bursting out laughing.

FIGARO: (*aside*) If only he were grieving for this one! . . .

COUNT: What! I can't take a step . . . (*To the* COUNTESS.) But let's forget this oddity; it might poison the pleasure I feel in finding you here.

COUNTESS: (*imitating* SUZANNE's *speech*) Did you hope so?

COUNT: After your clever note. (*He takes her hand*) You're trembling?

COUNTESS: I've been afraid.

COUNT: It was not to deprive you of the kiss that I took his. (*He kisses her on the forehead.*)

COUNTESS: Such liberties!

FIGARO: (*aside*) The hussy!

SUZANNE: (*aside*) The darling!

COUNT: (*takes his wife's hand*) But how fine and soft your skin is! The Countess's hand is not so lovely!

COUNTESS: (*aside*) What prejudice will do!

COUNT: Is her arm as firm and roundish, her pretty fingers as graceful and mischievous?

COUNTESS: (*in* SUZANNE's *voice*) How about love? . . .

COUNT: Love . . . is only the romance of the heart; pleasure is its history; it brings me to your feet.

COUNTESS: You don't love her any more?

COUNT: I love her very much, but three years' union makes marriage so respectable!

COUNTESS: What did you want from her?

COUNT: (*caressing her*) What I find in you, my sweet . . .

COUNTESS: Please tell me.

COUNT: . . . I don't know. Less sameness, perhaps; more spice in manner; a certain indefinable something that makes for charm; a refusal sometimes; I don't know. Our wives think all they have to do is to love us. They take it for granted, so they love us and love us . . . if they love us! . . . and they are so compliant and so constantly obliging, always and without respite, that suddenly one fine evening one finds satiety where one sought happiness.

COUNTESS: (*aside*) Oh, what a lesson!

COUNT: In truth, Suzy, I have often thought that if we seek elsewhere that pleasure we miss in them, it is because they do not study enough the art of sustaining our interest, of renewing their charm in love, of resurrecting, so to speak, the delight of possession by that of variety.

COUNTESS: (*offended*) So theirs is the entire responsibility?

COUNT: (*laughing*) And the man has none? Well, can we change nature? Our task is to obtain wives; theirs . . .

COUNTESS: And theirs?

COUNT: Is to keep us. That's overlooked too much.

COUNTESS: Not by me.

COUNT: Nor me.

FIGARO: (*aside*) Nor me.

SUZANNE: (*aside*) Nor me.

COUNT: (*takes his wife's hand*) There is an echo hereabouts; let's talk lower. You needn't worry about it, you whom Love has made so sprightly and so pretty! With a touch of caprice you would be the most fetching mistress! (*He kisses her forehead*) My Suzanne, a Castilian has only his word. Here is all the gold I promised to redeem that old claim I no longer have upon the delightful concession you are about to make me. But as the charm you condescend to put in it is priceless, I'll add this diamond, which you'll wear for love of me.

COUNTESS: (*curtsying*) Suzanne accepts everything.

FIGARO: (*aside*) They don't come more wanton than that.

SUZANNE: (*aside*) There's good money for us.

COUNT: (*aside*) She is mercenary; so much the better.

COUNTESS: (*turns toward the rear*) I see torches.

COUNT: They're the preparations for your wedding. Let's go for a moment into one of the pavilions to let them pass by?

COUNTESS: Without a light?

COUNT: (*drags her gently*) What's the use? We have nothing to read.

FIGARO: (*aside*) She's going in; well, I suspected as much. (*He steps forward.*)

COUNT: (*turning around, makes his voice threatening*) Who's passing there?

FIGARO: (*angry*) No one's passing; I'm coming on purpose!

COUNT: (*in a low voice to the* COUNTESS) It's Figaro! . . . (*He runs away.*)

COUNTESS: I'll follow you. (*She goes into the pavilion to her right while the* COUNT *hides in the woods in the rear.*)

SCENE 8

FIGARO, SUZANNE, *in the darkness*

FIGARO: (*tries to see where the* COUNT *and the* COUNTESS *go, whom he mistakes for* SUZANNE) I no longer hear anything, they must have entered. So here I am. (*In a changed voice*) You awkward husbands who hire spies and toy with suspicion for months without confirming it, why don't you imitate me? I follow my wife from the first day, and I listen. In a jiffy I know all; it's charming: no doubts left, one knows what to think. (*Walking briskly.*) Luckily it hardly bothers me and her treachery no longer upsets me. I have them at last!

SUZANNE: (*who has stepped forward softly in the darkness; aside*) You're going to pay for your fine suspicions. (*Imitating the* COUNTESS) Who goes there?

FIGARO: (*wild*) "Who goes there?" One who rightly believes the plague should have taken . . .

SUZANNE: (*in the* COUNTESS's *voice*) Why, it's Figaro!

FIGARO: (*looks and says quickly*) My lady Countess!

SUZANNE: Speak low.

FIGARO: (*quickly*) Ah! madam, Heaven sends you at the proper moment! Where do you think my lord may be?

SUZANNE: What does an ungrateful man matter to me? Tell me . . .

FIGARO: (*more rapidly*) And Suzanne, my bride, where do you think she may be?

SUZANNE: But speak low.

FIGARO: (*very quickly*) That Suzy who was thought so virtuous, who acted so modest! They're locked up in there. I'm going to call out.

SUZANNE: (*putting her hand on his mouth, forgets to disguise her voice*) Don't call out.

FIGARO: (*aside*) Why, it's Suzy! God-dam!

SUZANNE: (*in the* COUNTESS's *voice*) You seem uneasy.

FIGARO: (*aside*) The traitress! Trying to surprise me!

SUZANNE: We must avenge ourselves, Figaro.

FIGARO: Do you feel an urgent need for it?

SUZANNE: I would not be a woman! But men have a hundred means.

FIGARO: (*confidingly*) Madam, no one is intruding. Women's means . . . are worth them all.

SUZANNE: (*aside*) How I should like to slap him!

FIGARO: (*aside*) Wouldn't it be real fun if before the wedding! . . .

SUZANNE: But what kind of vengeance is it that a little love doesn't spice?

FIGARO: Wherever you see no signs, you can be sure that deference restrains one.

SUZANNE: (*offended*) I don't know whether you think it honestly, but you say it gracefully.

FIGARO: (*with comical fervor, kneeling*) Oh, madam, I adore you. But consider the time, the place, the circumstances, and let your resentment supply the grace which my entreaty lacks.

SUZANNE: (*aside*) My hand is itching.

FIGARO: (*aside*) My heart is beating.

SUZANNE: But, sir, have you reflected . . . ?

FIGARO: Yes, madam, oh, yes, I have reflected.

SUZANNE: . . . that in anger and in love . . .

FIGARO: . . . all delay is fatal. Your hand, madam?

SUZANNE: (*in her own voice and slapping him*) Here it is!

FIGARO: Satan, what a slap!

SUZANNE: (*slaps him again*) What slap? and this one?

FIGARO: Now, what the devil! Is this the day of raps?

SUZANNE: (*slaps him with each phrase*) "Ah, Satan, Suzanne." Take that for your suspicions and that for your vengeance, your treason, your schemes, your insults, and your plans. That's love for you! Say it then as you did this morning?

FIGARO: (*laughs as he gets up*) Saint Barbara, it is love! Oh happiness! Oh bliss! Oh many times blessed Figaro! Strike me, beloved, without stopping. But, only when you've mottled my body with bruises, look kindly, Suzy, upon the luckiest man ever beaten by a woman.

SUZANNE: *The luckiest.* You scoundrel, none the less you were seducing the Countess with your illusory babble to the point where, to tell the truth, I was forgetting myself and yielding for her.

FIGARO: Could I mistake the sound of your lovely voice?

SUZANNE: (*laughing*) You recognized me? Ah, how I'll take my vengeance for that!

FIGARO: Just like a woman to beat one and bear a grudge too! But tell me please by what stroke of luck I see you here when I thought you were with him; and why these clothes, which fooled me, now prove you innocent . . .

SUZANNE: You are the innocent one, to walk into a trap laid for another. Is it our fault if wanting to catch a fox we catch two?

FIGARO: So who's catching the other?

SUZANNE: His wife?

FIGARO: His wife!

SUZANNE: His wife.

FIGARO: (*madly*) Ah Figaro, go hang yourself; you never guessed that one! His wife? Oh clever, clever, clever women! So all the kisses of that room?

SUZANNE: Were given to madam.

FIGARO: And the one from the page?

SUZANNE: (*laughing*) To my lord.

FIGARO: And some time ago, behind the chair?

SUZANNE: To no one.

FIGARO: Are you sure?

SUZANNE: (*laughing*) Figaro, you know how slaps fly.

FIGARO: (*kisses her hand*) Yours are jewels to me. But the Count's was fair enough.

SUZANNE: Come, proud one, abase yourself!

FIGARO: (*acts as he speaks*) That's right: on my knee, bowed low, prone, and flat on the ground.

SUZANNE: (*laughing*) The poor Count! What trouble he's gone to . . .

FIGARO: (*rises on his knees*) . . . To seduce his wife!

SCENE 9

THE COUNT *enters from the rear of the stage and goes straight to the pavilion on his right;* FIGARO, SUZANNE

COUNT: (*to himself*) I am looking for her in the wood in vain; perhaps she has stepped in here.

SUZANNE: (*whispering to* FIGARO) It's he.

COUNT: (*opening the pavilion*) Suzy, are you there?

FIGARO: (*in a low voice*) He's looking for her and I thought . . .

SUZANNE: (*in a low voice*) He did not recognize her.

FIGARO: Let's finish him off, shall we? (*He kisses her hand.*)

COUNT: (*turns around*) A man kneeling before the Countess! . . . And I'm unarmed. (*He steps forward.*)

FIGARO: (*rises and disguises his voice*) Forgive me, madam, if I did not realize that this rendezvous would be in the path of the wedding festivities.

COUNT: (*aside*) That's the man of this morning in the dressing-room. (*He strikes his forehead.*)

FIGARO: But it will not be said that so silly an interference shall postpone our pleasure.

COUNT: (*aside*) Death and damnation!

FIGARO: (*leading her to the pavilion. In a low voice.*) He's cursing. (*aloud*) Let us hurry, madam, and repair the wrong we suffered earlier when I jumped out of the window.

COUNT: (*aside*) Ah, I see it all now.

SUZANNE: (*near the pavilion on her left*) Before we enter, make sure nobody is following. (*He kisses her on the forehead.*)

COUNT: (*shouts*) Vengeance! (SUZANNE *flees into the pavilion where* FANCHETTE, MARCELINE *and* CHÉRUBIN *have gone.*)

SCENE 10

THE COUNT, FIGARO

(*The* COUNT *seizes* FIGARO *by the arm.*)

COUNT: (*recognizes him*) Ah! villain, it's you! Ho there, somebody, come at once!

SCENE 11

PÉDRILLE, THE COUNT, FIGARO

PÉDRILLE: (*booted*) My lord, I find you at last.

COUNT: Good, it's Pédrille! Are you alone?

PÉDRILLE: Back from Seville, at breakneck speed.

COUNT: Come close to me and shout very loud.

PÉDRILLE: (*shouting at the top of his voice*) No more

page in Seville than on my hand. That's all.

COUNT: (*pushes him away*) You loon!

PÉDRILLE: My lord told me to shout.

COUNT: (*still holding* FIGARO) It was to call for help. Ho there, somebody! Whoever hears me, come quickly.

PÉDRILLE: Figaro and I are two; what can be happening to you?

SCENE 12

THE PRECEDING ACTORS, BRID'OISON, BARTHOLO, BAZILE, ANTONIO, GRIPPE-SOLEIL

(*The whole wedding party hastens up with torches.*)

BARTHOLO: (*to* FIGARO) You see we came at your first signal . . .

COUNT: (*pointing to the pavilion on his left*) Pédrille, seize that door. (PÉDRILLE *goes.*)

BAZILE: (*in a low voice to* FIGARO) You surprised him with Suzanne?

COUNT: (*pointing to* FIGARO) All of you, my vassals, surround this man and answer for him with your lives.

BAZILE: Ha! ha!

COUNT: (*furious*) Please be quiet! (*To* FIGARO *in a freezing tone*) My knight, will you reply to my questions?

FIGARO: (*coldly*) Who indeed could give me leave not to, my lord? You command everybody here except yourself.

COUNT: (*restraining himself*) Except myself!

ANTONIO: That's the way to talk.

COUNT: (*gets angry again*) No, if anything could make me more furious, it is the calm air he assumes.

FIGARO: Are we soldiers killing and being killed for interests they don't know? For my part, I want to know why I'm angry.

COUNT: (*beside himself*) Oh, rage! (*Controlling himself.*) Man of gentle birth who feign not to know, would you at least do us the favor of telling us what lady you have brought into this pavilion?

FIGARO: (*mischievously pointing to the other*) Into that one?

COUNT: (*quickly*) Into this one.

FIGARO: (*coldly*) That's different. It's a young lady who honors me with her favors.

BAZILE: (*astonished*) Ha! ha!

COUNT: (*quickly*) You heard him, gentlemen?

BARTHOLO: (*astonished*) We heard him.

COUNT: (*to* FIGARO) And the young person has no other ties that you know of?

FIGARO: (*coldly*) I know that a great lord paid her some attentions for a while; but whether he neglected her or she likes me better than one who is more lovable, I am the one preferred.

COUNT: (*quickly*) The one pref—(*Restraining himself*) At least he is naïf! For what he has admitted, gentlemen, I have heard, I swear, from the very mouth of his accomplice.

BRID'OISON: (*stupefied*) His ac-complice.

COUNT: (*in fury*) Now, when dishonor is public, so must be the revenge!

(*He goes into the pavilion.*)

SCENE 13

ALL THE PRECEDING ACTORS, *except the Count*

ANTONIO: It's right.

BRID'OISON: (*to* FIGARO) So who took who-o-o's wife?

FIGARO: (*laughing*) No one had that pleasure.

SCENE 14

THE PRECEDING ACTORS, THE COUNT, CHÉRUBIN

COUNT: (*speaking from inside the pavilion and tugging at someone that he does not see as yet*) All your efforts are useless, madam, you are doomed and your hour has struck! (*He comes out without looking*) How unfortunate that there is no pledge of a union so detested . . .

FIGARO: (*calls out*) Chérubin!

COUNT: My page?

BAZILE: Ha! ha!

COUNT: (*beside himself, aside*) Always the confounded page! (*To* CHÉRUBIN) What were you doing in that room?

CHÉRUBIN: (*shyly*) I was hiding, as you ordered me to.

PÉDRILLE: It wasn't worth while nearly killing a horse!

COUNT: You go in there, Antonio: bring before her judge the criminal who has dishonored me.

BRID'OISON: Is it madam that you are l-looking for?

ANTONIO: It's Providence, by gum, for all you've done over the countryside! . . .

COUNT: (*furious*) Go in there! (ANTONIO *enters.*)

SCENE 15

THE PRECEDING ACTORS, *except Antonio*

COUNT: You're going to see, gentlemen, that the page was not alone.

CHÉRUBIN: (*shyly*) My lot would have been too cruel if some gentle soul had not sweetened its bitterness.

SCENE 16

THE PRECEDING ACTORS, ANTONIO, FANCHETTE

ANTONIO: (*pulling by the arm someone who can't be seen as yet*) Come, madam, don't make me coax you since everybody knows you went in.

FIGARO: (*calls out*) My little cousin!

BAZILE: Ha! ha!

COUNT: Fanchette!

ANTONIO: (*turns around and exclaims*) Ah! by jiminy, it was right sharp of you, my lord, to pick me to show the company it was my daughter caused all that fuss!

COUNT: (*indignant*) Who could know she was in there? (*He wants to go in.*)

BARTHOLO: (*interposing*) Allow me, my lord; all this is not clearer. Perhaps I can deal with it in cold blood. (*He goes in.*)

BRID'OISON: It's surely too c-confusing for me.

SCENE 17

THE PRECEDING ACTORS, MARCELINE

BARTHOLO: (*speaking from within and coming out*) Fear nothing, madam, no harm will come to you. I vouch for it. (*He turns around and cries out*) Marceline! . . .

BAZILE: Ha! ha!

FIGARO: What a madhouse! My mother's in it too?

ANTONIO: They vie in doing the worst.

COUNT: (*indignant*) What do I care? The Countess . . .

SCENE 18

THE PRECEDING ACTORS, SUZANNE

(SUZANNE, *her face behind a fan.*)

COUNT: . . . Ah, there she is! (*He takes her violently by the arm.*) What do you believe, gentlemen, such an odious . . . deserves? (SUZANNE *falls on her knees, bowing her head.*)

COUNT: Never, never. (FIGARO *kneels on the other side.*)

COUNT: (*louder*) Never, never. (MARCELINE *kneels before him.*)

COUNT: (*louder*) Never, never. (*They all kneel, except* BRID'OISON.)

COUNT: (*beside himself*) Never, even if there were a hundred of you!

SCENE 19 AND LAST

ALL THE PRECEDING ACTORS, THE COUNTESS *comes out of the other pavilion*

COUNTESS: (*kneels*) At least, I can make one more.

COUNT: (*looking at the* COUNTESS *and at* SUZANNE) Ah! What do I see?

BRID'OISON: (*laughing*) Why, it's madam.

COUNT: (*wants to lift up the* COUNTESS) What! It was you, Countess? (*In a supplicating tone.*) Only a very generous forgiveness . . .

COUNTESS: (*laughing*) You would say in my place "Never, never"; but I, for the third time today, forgive you unconditionally. (*She gets up.*)

SUZANNE: (*gets up*) And so do I.

MARCELINE: (*gets up*) So do I.

FIGARO: (*gets up*) So do I. There's an echo hereabouts. (*They all get up.*)

COUNT: An echo!—I wanted to use trickery with them and they treated me like a child!

COUNTESS: (*laughing*) Don't be sorry, my lord.

FIGARO: (*brushing off his knees with his hat*) A day like today is good training for an ambassador!

COUNT: (*to* SUZANNE) That note sealed with a pin?

SUZANNE: Madam dictated it.

COUNT: The reply is long overdue. (*He kisses the* COUNTESS's *hand.*)

COUNTESS: Each will get his own. (*She gives the purse to* FIGARO *and the diamond to* SUZANNE.)

SUZANNE: (*to* FIGARO) Still another dowry.

FIGARO: (*striking the purse in his hand*) And three. This one was hard to get!

SUZANNE: Like our marriage.

GRIPPE-SOLEIL: What about the bride's garter? May I have it?

COUNTESS: (*takes out the ribbon she has kept so long in*

her bosom and throws it on the ground) The garter? It was in her clothes; here it is. (*The boys of the wedding party want to pick it up.*)

CHÉRUBIN: (*more alert, runs to pick it up and says*) Would the one that wants it come and get it from me!

COUNT: (*laughing, to the page*) For such a touchy gentleman, what did you find so funny in the slap I gave you?

CHÉRUBIN: (*goes backwards as he half draws his sword*) Me, colonel?

FIGARO: (*comically angry*) He got it on my cheek: that is how lords mete out justice!

COUNT: (*laughing*) On your cheek? Ha! ha! ha! What do you say to that, dear Countess?

COUNTESS: (*absorbed, returns to reality and says feelingly*) Indeed, dear Count, I do, and for life, I swear it, and no inadvertence.

COUNT: (*slapping the judge on the shoulder*). And you, Brid'oison, let us have your opinion.

BRID'OISON: On everything I s-see, my lord? . . . Well, my opinion is that I d-don't know what to say: that's my way of thinking.

ALL: (*together*) A sound judgment.

FIGARO: I was poor and despised. When I showed some cleverness, hatred pursued me. A pretty girl and some money . . .

BARTHOLO: (*laughing*) People are going to swarm around you.

FIGARO: It is possible?

BARTHOLO: I know them.

FIGARO: (*bowing to the spectators*) Aside from my wife and my property, you are all welcome to what I have. (*The orchestra plays the ritornelle of the song. A well-known tune.*)

SONG

BAZILE:

FIRST COUPLET

> Triple dowry, handsome wife,
> Is all that a husband needs!
> 'Gainst a lord or a beardless page
> Only a fool feels jealous rage.
> Let the Latin proverb bless
> What man gets from this life.

FIGARO: Don't I know it . . . (*He sings.*) *Gaudeant bene nati.*

BAZILE: No . . . (*He sings.*) *Gaudeant bene* nanti.[2]

SUZANNE:

SECOND COUPLET

> Let a man his wife betray,
> He boasts of it, all are gay;
> Let his wife indulge her whim,
> She is punished, unlike him.
> This injustice is absurd,

[2] *Gaudeant bene nati* is the Latin for "Happy those of noble birth"; *gaudeant bene nanti*, Bazile's version, means "Happy those who swim well." It should be *nantes*.

Do you ask why this is so?
It's the stronger's vicious law . . .   (*Encore.*)

FIGARO:

THIRD COUPLET

John Mc John, the jealous boor,
Wanted to have both wife and rest;
Hired a most awful dog
And left him in the garden.
At night, what a frightful din!
All are bitten by the beast,
Save the lover from whom leased . . .   (*Encore.*)

THE COUNTESS:

FOURTH COUPLET

Some wives are proud and prudish,
They do not love their husbands;
Others, though, nearly rakish,
Swear they love no one but him;
Now the worthiest are those,
Never swearing this or that,
Who merely strive for chastity . . .   (*Encore.*)

THE COUNT:

FIFTH COUPLET

A woman of the provinces
Who believes in duty strict
In romance has no success
I prefer one who's derelict!
Like a piece of currency,
Stamped with one man's effigy,
But serving the needs of all . . .   (*Encore.*)

MARCELINE:

SIXTH COUPLET

Everyone his mother knows,
Her who gave her life for him.
All the rest is only dim.
How else explain love's secret?

FIGARO *breaks in*:

This secret may disclose
How the offspring of a boor
Is worth his weight in gold . . .   (*Encore.*)

SEVENTH COUPLET

By the accident of birth,
One is shepherd, one is king;
Chance made lord and underling;
Only the mind can change all.
Of twenty kings fed on praise
All in death are common earth,
While Voltaire immortal stays! . . .   (*Encore.*)

CHÉRUBIN:

EIGHTH COUPLET

Beloved sex, fickle sex,
You who torment all our days,
If each one complains of you
In the end they all come back.
The pit, though, is your image:
Such a one professes scorn
Who would crawl to earn your praise . . .

(*Encore.*)

SUZANNE:

NINTH COUPLET

If there should a moral be
In this mad, this cheerful work,
For the sake of gaiety,
Please forgive us if you will.
Thus does Nature sensibly
Lead us, in our desires
To her goal, by pleasure . . .   (*Encore.*)

BRID'OISON:

TENTH COUPLET

Now, dear sirs, the c-comedy
You're judging in t-this moment
Apes the l-life of all of you
Sitting there and listening.
When annoyed, you storm and shout,
But altogether you mutter l-long,
All we d-do just ends in s-song . . .   (*Encore.*)

GENERAL BALLET

SELECTED BIBLIOGRAPHY

(Biography and Criticism of Beaumarchais)

Bailly, A. *Beaumarchais*, Paris, 1945.

Bettelheim, A. *Beaumarchais. Eine Biographie.* Munich, 1911.

Cordier, H. *Bibliographie des œuvres de Beaumarchais.* Paris, 1883.

Dalsème, R. *La Vie de Beaumarchais.* Paris, 1928. (Eng. tr., 1929)

Frischauer, P. *Beaumarchais, der Abenteuer im Jahrhundert der Frauen.* Zurich, 1935. (Eng. tr., 1935)

Guitry, S. *Beaumarchais.* Paris, 1950.

Hall, Evelyn B. *The Friends of Voltaire.* London, 1906.

Hallays, A. *Beaumarchais.* Paris, 1897.

Hazard, Blanche E. *Beaumarchais and the American Revolution.* Boston, 1910.

Hewlett, M. "Beaumarchais," in *Cornhill Magazine,* N.S., LIV (1923).

Kite, Elizabeth S. *Beaumarchais and the War of American Independence.* 2v. Boston, 1918.

Langley, E. F. "Introduction" to his edition of *Le Mariage de Figaro.* New York-London, 1917.

Lanson, G. *Histoire de la littérature française.* 19th ed. Paris, 1926.

Latzarus, L. *Beaumarchais.* Paris, 1930.

Lemaître, G. E. *Beaumarchais.* New York, 1949.

Lescure, M. F. D. de. *Etude sur Beaumarchais.* Paris, 1887.

Lintilhac, E. *Beaumarchais et ses œuvres*. Paris, 1884.

Loménie, L. L. de. *Beaumarchais et son temps*. 2v. Paris, 1856.
(Eng. tr., 1859)

Rivers, J. *Figaro: the Life of Beaumarchais*. London, 1922.